HAPPY BABIES SWIM

ULRIKA FAERCH

HAPPY BABIES SWIM

Creating stronger relationships between parents
and children through the gift of swim

Contents

To my Dad who gave me the gift of swim

Foreword

This book is a brilliant example of how instructive and uplifting it can be when experienced, dedicated people share their wisdom. On the one hand, it will teach you everything worth knowing about baby swimming, but at the same time you can learn a lot from it about being an attentive and *present* parent.

It's been barely a generation since it became apparent to us how important the relationship between parent and child is. We used to call it *interaction*; now it's the *relationship*, and the child's first four years' worth has been demonstrated to lay the groundwork for the connection between parent and child in the long term.

In our frequent talk about attachment as something important for children's well-being and development, we often forget to emphasize that it works both ways: The better the connection and the richer the relationship, the more the parents also thrive and develop. Doing things together is the best way to build a strong relationship, and that applies not only to parents and children but between the parents themselves. Where adults and older children can bond through language, baby swimming provides a brilliant joint activity for parents and children who aren't talking yet. More than just an end in itself, the activity takes place in the context of building mutual trust, instilling a sense of security that can be more difficult to create later.

For most babies, swimming is a pleasant experience. That's not always the case with other common chores, such as changing diapers or bathing, but the interaction in baby swimming can teach parents a lot about how to follow the child's body language and moods in other activities as well, without sacrificing responsibility and leadership. This helps build a shared reserve of happy, harmonious experiences that can come in handy at those times when parents and children are not perfectly in sync.

—Jesper Juul, Danish internationally renowned family therapist and author

Introduction

What if I told you, I could help guide you and your family to find more balance, achieve a higher degree of resilience, and grow towards a stronger bond together?

And what if you could do all this through the fun activity of swimming?

If you are like thousands of others from around the globe, you may be cheering "sign me up!"

Swimming is an activity that promotes grace, fluidity and inner calm. But it's also FUN! It can be done in oceans, lakes, rivers and pools—all around the world.

Many cultures start incorporating swimming into babies' routines from an early age. Some cultures, however, are fearful of baby swimming due to insecurity, lack of knowledge and a mix of bad experiences that may be personal, or stories told by other people that had a bad experience whether it is a current situation or from a previous generation. I want to change any negative stigma around baby swimming and shine a positive light on the many ways it can lead to a **happier baby and happier family.**

As an experienced competitive swimmer myself, I have a personal and professional connection with the water. I am so confident in the transformative powers that water has, and the act of swimming, that I have built my entire life around it!

In this book, I share stories from families I have worked with through the years, and explain how their personal swim journeys can help guide your own family as you learn from their mistakes and triumphs. By highlighting different scenarios, I will help coach you and explain the cognitive, emotional and physical advantages that swimming may bring by building a stronger relationship between the child and their parents or caregiver. *Note: the stories in this book are based on families from Swimmix, the swim school I founded and operated in Sweden and Denmark for more than 20 years, as well as various swim schools around the world where I have provided counsel on the baby swim programs. All stories are based on real interactions, but have been altered to protect privacy.*

My goal in writing this book is to inspire families, around the world, to get into the water, with your baby, and swim!

This book is a guide to swimming with babies age newborn to two-years-old, with an emphasis on how families can use swim to foster healthier and happier relationships. Many of the themes I'll share can be mastered in the water and then applied in everyday life on land.

Part 1 focuses on how family swim can lead to a much healthier and stronger relationship between everyone involved. Topics include an array of developmental growth that can lead to emotional, social and relational advancements, with the pool helping you and your baby flourish. This section is the groundwork for what you need to know and understand, before getting into the water, so that your experience can be the happiest that it can be, together with your baby.

Part 2 is about the logistics for prepping for swim time and recommended swim activities for once you're in the water. I provide examples of activities and various ways for you to support your baby, while swimming as a family. These are taken from my years of experience and represent the most useful and effective activities to teach your baby how to swim in a healthy way, with you by your baby's side. I share techniques and remind you of how the relationship and emotional intelligence discussed in Part 1 relates to it all.

As with anything, all babies and parents (or other caregivers reading this) are different. Please use this book as a guide. Listen to yourself, and listen to your child. Together, with the wonders of water and the gift of swimming, we will have a wonderful time splashing around and strengthening your family dynamic.

Let's dive in!

– Ulrika

Chapter 1

"If you want others to be happy,
practice compassion. If you want to be
happy, practice compassion."
– Dalai Lama

My Story

In my earlier years as a swim teacher, I thought we teachers and parents were dealing with a very common developmental stage: separation anxiety. When I approached a family in the water, some children would turn their heads away from me, while clinging to their parents. Gently, we would turn the baby so I was standing behind the child and holding them under their arms so they continued to face their parents. Parents would quickly give the baby a submerging cue and I would dip the baby under the water, letting them swim underwater back to the parent. Parents were always impressed and the babies appeared to be okay, but something felt off.

As time went on, I noticed that certain babies built up a resistance towards me as we had started the submersion activities in class.

Being submerged always happened only a few weeks into swim classes. At this point in time I hadn't fully developed my eye towards reading the sensitivities and nuances of a baby's comfort. Back then, being submerged was a central idea to baby swimming in my swim school, and most other schools around the world, so a lot of exercises and techniques were built around this skill. Having the babies go underwater was part of a "wow" moment, and the class curriculum was skill-based.

As time went on, I noticed an unfortunate pattern. Every time a new group of swimmers reached this point in their learning, their behavior would change towards me and when their parents gave them a cue to go underwater some would become upset. Before submersion, the babies seemed to be enjoying swim class and happy to see me. Now they were showing unease before dipping under the water and were tense around me. I thought to myself, "something is wrong. I need to figure this out."

Changing My Vantage Point

I spent a lot of time mulling the problem over. Why were some babies suddenly resistant and why did they react to me so anxiously (all of a sudden)? Could there be more happening beyond separation anxiety from their parents?

That's when I started looking at the situation from a new angle. I shifted my point of view from my own eyes, to the babies eyes, and suddenly everything became clear. The problem was not merely some developmental phase they had reached where they wanted their parents. The problem was my teaching methods.

I had always seen myself as the "good, funny, playful" teacher, but from the babies' point of view I had become the "mean lady" who took them from their parents and dunked them underwater! If they'd been able to talk when I approached them, the babies might have said, "No, thanks. This is not fun. This seems to be more fun for you and my parents than for me! I don't like this. I'm a person too—please listen to me! I'll tell you when this feels meaningful to me too, but it's not by doing it this way."

When I think about those days, I wish I knew then what I know now. But I didn't get it right away and the parents didn't understand that anything more than separation anxiety was at play either. Maybe we were so caught up in the submerging skill that we lost sight of the babies themselves and their feelings.

I will always wish that I recognized the importance of "tuning-in" sooner and making the experience meaningful for the babies. Through the lessons I learned, I am very pleased you can learn from my mistakes.

An Appropriate, Empathetic Response

In my case, the babies who appeared uneasy, or who became slightly rigid in their body language—some clinging to their parents—were trying to tell us something beyond, "I just want my Mommy (or Daddy!)," but I didn't pick up on it. In my class the children had become objects and the submerging exercise became the goal of being in the water—the *piece de resistance* of baby swim school. Not truly understanding the babies' reactions and needs, I was focused on the skill itself and it left some babies feeling stressed and unhappy. Once I recognized the problem, I changed my approach. I researched and read everything I could find on baby development and rewrote the entire curriculum.

Rather than emphasizing skills and exercises, my swim program now focused on how babies learn—in the context of a relationship. It became about the babies and their parents' emotional experience: how it felt to the child, the babies' readiness to be in a new environment and the parents' readiness and responsiveness to their baby. I also realized that the parents were as much my students as the babies were. As the teacher,

I began to watch (and teach the parents to watch) for nuanced communications from their babies and to react to them in an empathic way. Rather than focus on reaching physical milestones through the activities of swimming, I realized that swimming milestones came to each baby in their own time. The priority of each class became about the experience of swimming together, with the caregiver and baby learning about each other and themselves, through swim.

I gave it a lot of thought and was so happy to discover that there are few activities in life that can foster relationships as well as swimming can. Swimming lessons can become the catalyst that leads to much deeper and more important life lessons.

My goal became creating a safe, predictable and supportive swim school environment where both parents and children grew stronger—through empathetic guiding. This built incredible trust between parents and babies, as well as everyone in the swim group.

To be clear, every baby goes through a phase of separation anxiety, at one time or another, and that was undoubtedly an influence on this situation. Saying that, when I changed the approach to our swim classes, the babies' behaviors changed too. From the moment we began to see and treat the children as equals, with needs of their own, I was transformed from the "Dunking Monster" to being what I always wished for— *the trustworthy and supportive teacher who created a learning environment where everyone felt equally important and valued, leading to fun for all!*

The parents and babies were becoming a team and my teachers and I had a renewed focus to carefully respect each student "partnership" in an individualized way. Parents learned how they could support their baby's development and were encouraged to respect their baby's personal space and mood. For example, if a baby was not in the mood to swim, it was encouraged to step back and simply hold your baby while watching others, or even leave early if it was simply too much for that day.

With the babies happier, the parents had a more positive experience too. Everyone relaxed more and was able to be present. The entire energy of the pool changed to a happier vibe. As for the babies, not only did they no longer turn their eyes and bodies away from me, but they kept seeking eye contact and some babies even began to reach for me in class. Once they were ready to submerge, they showed excitement when they knew the submerging portion of class was coming. They said in their own way, "I'm ready now and can't wait to do this!"

As my group of teachers and I got better at guiding parents into making the swim activities meaningful to the babies, on their terms, the babies' natural curiosity and joy bubbled up once again. I learned so much from this experience, but the key lessons include:

- **If you want a relationship built on trust, never trick or push someone to do something they are not ready to do.**
- **Trust and joy can't be forced. They need to truly come from within, no matter how young or old a person may be.**
- **It is the adult's responsibility, as the leader, to ensure that baby swimming indeed has the baby as the priority over anything else!**

Happy Babies Swim

Every parent wants their baby to be happy. Whether you are a first-time parent, or have multiple children, this book can help you make your baby, that is still getting adjusted to their world, happy. If your baby is already happy, then it will help you make him even happier. My model for doing this, through swim, is by focusing on building a strong relationship between you and your baby.

The Harvard Study of Adult Development, did an almost 80 year study that found "close relationships, more than money or fame, are what keep people happy throughout their lives."

Water is fascinating. It makes up about 70% of Earth and yet water is much more of a mystery to us than land. We also spend nine months (give or take) surrounded in water (amniotic fluid) before we are born, and we have contact with the water throughout life in multiple ways. This makes water a very natural environment for humans—we are drawn to it.

The gift of swimming is an extremely powerful activity for parents and babies to share. Swimming is wonderful for any age. In this book, however, I hone in on swimming with babies up to two-years of age.

In talking to parents and other colleagues from around the world, much of the hesitation around baby swimming has to do with people's lack of knowledge or understanding of the benefits, their own bad experiences, or how it has been taught in a way that doesn't respect the integrity of the baby (i.e., the baby's emotions and feelings are disregarded). If we are not mindful, baby swimming can become skill-based with a tactical approach, with the baby as the sole student.

What is better, and what I teach, is a baby-centric model that focuses on listening to your baby's communication and respecting the integrity of the baby. My teachings also focus on the relationship between the baby and you.

In my classes, it is the parents (or other caregivers) swimming with their babies who are the primary students. The reason for this is that the adult must take responsibility and be the leader when guiding a baby. If the adult is not learning and growing in their relationship knowledge and skills, how can a baby learn and grow? By teaching in this way, not only is the emotional relationship between you and your baby understood better—by both parties—but there is also a positive change towards growth and development because you and your baby are on equal ground (or in this case equal water!). You are a team, learning together.

In this way, when families start participating in baby swim classes—or swimming at home using the lessons in this book—there is a longer runway for a healthy, happy relationship right from the earliest days of your baby's life.

Trust is the foundation for learning, growth and healthy relationships. Water creates vulnerability that can trigger emotions, and through close proximity of being together with your child, as you swim together, you can build mutual trust and become more synchronized.

As you practice swimming, you are really practicing a range of life skills including self awareness, control, focus, planning and flexibility. As these lessons unfold gracefully in the water, you will begin to understand your child better, they will understand you better and you will work together towards a happy, healthy bond that lasts in the water, and also on land.

Often, the "race for achievement" (Did my child succeed? Did they do it better / faster than the others?) can affect the relationship between a parent and baby. The parent becomes insecure and questions if they are doing everything "right" and spends time worrying about the baby reaching milestones "on time" instead of being present and progressing at the baby's pace. More often than not, your little one will reach cognitive and motor skill milestones when they are ready, in their time. Your job is to tune-in to your baby's needs to provide a sense of security and confidence, showing them patience and positive energy that exudes support, trust and love.

My teaching is about the quality of the relationship. Guiding parents to become more emotionally aware, learning *with* their baby and *growing together as a team*. In teaching baby swimming this way, it directly leads to a healthier and happier family dynamic and also enhances learning.

Swimming together can start with a simple bath. A bathtub is a wonderful place for you and your baby to first become comfortable together in the water. With your newborn, a bath offers a controlled environment that feels safe. In your loving arms, you and your baby can move through different movements and experience the water in a way that will transcend your bath-time routine into something much more meaningful.

For most parents reading this book, with babies that are 3 months or older, a pool—likely an indoor pool depending on the time of year—is where you and your baby will take your swimming to the next level. A pool offers plenty of room for curious babies to explore, in your arms, as you both glide through the water and learn more about the water, yourselves, and each other, together.

Water, and the gift of swim, has so many benefits—emotional, relational, cognitive and physical. In fact, a 2012 study by *Robyn Jorgensen, at Griffith University, surveyed 7,000 parents from Australia, New Zealand and the United States, over the course of four years, and found that "children who learn how to swim at a young age are reaching many developmental milestones earlier than normal."*

Here's a quick look at some of the benefits you and your baby can likely expect to see when swimming together.

To maximize the benefits of baby swimming, I highly encourage you to swim with your baby and have it be a joint activity and experience. Most swim schools will offer you this opportunity, but there are some places that only let the baby take part. I strongly encourage you to find a swim school, or private pool, where you can swim together. If this isn't possible, the next best thing is to have your baby swim with someone that you trust and who you, and your baby, are comfortable with.

Emotional/Relational Benefits of Swimming

- Swimming is a universal activity that all generations can partake in.
- Water offers a range of experiences that evoke many emotions. By becoming more emotionally aware of your feelings and learning the feelings of your baby, you embark on a journey towards growth together.
- Swimming as a family allows people to learn how to respect the integrity of everyone's feelings in the water and tune-in to how the family can work together to achieve goals, while also facing challenging situations as a team. This builds self-esteem, confidence and trust.
- Swimming with your baby allows you and your baby to be at eye-level, which promotes bonding, trust and secure attachments. This quality time can also lead to healthier and happier relationships overall.

Physical Benefits of Swimming

- Water supports your child's weight, allowing your baby to move more freely, which is often a challenge on land during early months.
- Swimming together gives your baby a safe space to explore the feelings of buoyancy and balance that can stimulate and improve many motor skills. This exploration may start in the water, but the curiosity and willingness to try may carry over on land, which can lead to wonderful growth.
- Water offers resistance, which will build strength for your little one and support motor skill development through various swimming movements.
- Swimming offers your child a place to practice many motor skills that are challenging on land, providing your baby a chance to accelerate physical development through trial and error.

Cognitive Benefits of Swimming

- Water offers an environment that is likely free of technology and other distractions, allowing undivided attention between you and your baby. Your focused presence and the attention your baby will receive is invaluable to your relationship and emotional and cognitive growth.
- Water is ever changing. Depending on your behavior or attitude that day (and your baby's), the water may offer something new, challenging and fun each time you swim. This may create the foundation for both of you to learn how to adapt and instill a go-with-the-flow attitude in other areas of life too.
- Swimming together, especially in a class environment, offers the opportunity to help your child develop executive functions. Executive functions are skills for life such as focused thinking, how to limit and filter out distractions, sharing with others and emotional/impulse control to name a few. These skills are not innate, rather, they are developed and learned best in safe, predictable and happy environments with a trusted leader (like yourself!) helping to guide the baby.

Your baby is genetically programmed to feel safest and learn the best from the primary attachment caregivers. Together, you'll develop and learn, building a strong relationship that is healthy and happy!

You may be thinking "but I do *everything* together with my baby!" Not quite.

In most instances you are doing something *to* your baby—walking your baby in the stroller, tickling your baby, singing to your baby, swinging your baby, carrying your baby, feeding your baby, etc. You are the clear driver and in full control of these activities. Swimming allows you to do something *with* your baby and make it into an activity where you are both equal, even though you are the loving supportive leader.

The gift of swim can bring new happiness and a deeper level of understanding among those swimming together. This happens because swimming can reduce stress and increase serotonin (which makes a person feel significant) and oxytocin (the "love hormone," which is essential for building strong bonds). The best part about swimming with your baby is that because this activity can start at the newborn age, you and your child learn to have a healthier relationship and can develop a strong emotional connection right from the start.

Chapter 2

"Promise me you'll always remember:
You're braver than you believe, and stronger
than you seem, and smarter than you think."
Christopher Robin to Pooh—A.A. Milne

Children's Actions
Are Always Meaningful

Adults used to dictate everything. Many parents reading this book may have parents themselves that were raised during the "children should be seen and not heard" days. During the 1950s-1970s it was highly acceptable for children to "know their place" (whatever that means!) and if they weren't "doing as they should," they'd be disciplined accordingly. Many times this discipline hurt the child's core self and lacked understanding instead of showing support. That support is crucial to help babies grow into adults who are strong, empathetic beings with a high self-esteem and ability to navigate life well.

Today, parents are much more open-minded. They understand the world in a different way and seek harmony and emotional intelligence when raising their child. A parent today wants to "tune-in" and put themselves in their baby's shoes. They understand that if their baby is crying then something is wrong. Similarly, if their baby is smiling then something is right! Parents today are becoming more aware that they can help create more smiles with love than anything else.

By understanding that a child's actions have meaning, a parent can not only identify a problem and solve it faster, but a parent will also instill deep emotional confidence and trust between them and their baby.

Daniel N. Stern was a prominent American psychiatrist and psychoanalytic theorist specializing in infant development, and author of many books—most notably *The Interpersonal World of the Infant* (1985). He was a trailblazer in child development, sharing that an infant's actions are always meaningful and that learning to understand them requires careful listening and responsiveness. The best we can do is to try and understand what a child is attempting to communicate and the need behind it. Whether he is silent through body language (squirm, turn of the head, eyes widening) or cries a vocal plee (grunt, cry, squeal), babies are trying to tell us something—but what?!

Practically speaking, parents who believe that every one of their baby's actions has meaning are able to help guide their children towards comfort and happiness. Children develop an understanding that when they communicate to their parents, their parents will listen and respond to needs, which helps build their inner compass. The inner compass is a person's emotional guide towards a healthy, happy life. Our inner compass works best when we are in-tune with and understand our emotions and feelings because it helps to guide us towards what we need. When our inner compass is out of tune we might use self soothing techniques and become self-destructive (over-eating, starving, violent, abusive, etc.)

Through my years as a counselor and swim teacher, I also realized that the cause of the baby's reaction is not always what we may think it is. As parents or teachers, it's important to be wise enough to know that you may not always be right. If a child continues to be upset after you think you've found the solution, look further.

Your Child Needs You

Alan Sroufe, a Developmental Psychologist at the Institute for Child Development at the University of Minnesota, shared that "over the last 80 years, developmental scientists have come to understand that some micro-dynamics that take place between a baby and an adult in a caring relationship have a lifelong effect, in very specific ways, on the person that baby will become."

Babies are very astute in knowing when and if their parent, or caregiver, means what they are saying or doing. It's incredible that they are capable of picking up on whether or not the saying or action has heart behind it, and depending, a baby will respond accordingly. Micro-dynamics is the honest exchange between you and your baby. For example, if you are playing with your baby, but are distracted (either visably or through your thoughts), your baby can feel that you are not as interested in play as she is at that moment. A baby can also feel when you are fully invested and enjoying playtime as much as they are. That's not to say a parent has to be "on 24/7"—that isn't realistic. Even by respecting your baby and voicing, "I am tired today. We were up a lot last night, together, weren't we? Mama and Dada need to relax a little while you play, right now. okay?," you are explaining a truth and, through micro-dynamics, your baby is able to understand on some level. Likely, your baby will respond to this in a positive way.

Children need leadership that is proactive, caring, responsive and flexible in order to develop and thrive. Your child needs a safe, caring, reliable adult who picks up on his physical and emotional needs. When the child knows you are taking care of him and taking responsibility for his well-being, he'll relax easier.

Never believe in the old belief that a child is making a fuss just to be "fussy." A baby, newborn to 24 months of age does not know how to *act*. Babies are pure, honest and direct. With acceptance, understanding and adequate help from you, your baby will sooner be ready to move on from whatever is bothering him (because you've helped him fix the problem!) and again explore the world around him with basic trust, curiosity and joy. That problem can range from a variety of things—being tired, needing a new diaper, wanting a new activity—and as your relationship grows, you will be able to pick-up on cues faster, providing happiness to your baby most of the time. Of course, your baby will be upset from time to time, so go easy on yourself and your peanut. Situations such as teething, growing pains or a cold all play into a child's mood and behavior, but even being wise enough to know that your baby is having a tough time can help you and your baby be a team to get through challenging moments together.

Being a child takes energy. The excitement of every new little adventure, whether it's learning a new skill, joining a new swim school or meeting new people, all uses energy. At some point your baby may get so wound up that she needs to be in your arms to just relax, as you are her safe haven. Once your angel feels calm and recharged, her inborn curiosity will draw her back to *want* to discover more. Appropriate care in times of dependence will foster her independence and will show her how to explore both sides.

Stress in Babies

Babies and young children are very sensitive to stress. Researchers tell us that too much stress early in life can be toxic, disrupting brain development and causing problems with learning, behavior and both physical and mental health.

In the first year, it's important to address a babies' needs quickly, helping them move from discomfort to comfort. This establishes an understanding between you and your baby that you care and can be trusted. It has a positive effect on brain development, health and learning and it lays the early foundation for resilience.

That doesn't mean they should never feel discomfort or frustration—being hungry, tired, meeting new people—can all be stresses. There will also be situations we can not figure out—but that's okay. Our children have room for error to occur in their lives and it can be good lessons, too. If we react in a caring way, it actually helps build a tolerance for stresses down the road, because the child begins to feel assured that things will be okay.

How you react—and respond—is invaluable in building the foundation for a happy, balanced baby, that will grow up to be a happy, balanced adult.

In the water, dipping a child underwater (when neither of you is ready for it) will cause stress, so don't do it. Instead, guide your child with empathy in the pool, and on land. Going with your baby's curiosity to explore, or using gentle ways to introduce the underwater world to your child, will guarantee he enjoys it without jeopardizing the bond of trust between you.

Finding the Right Balance

While Millennial Parents (born between 1981 and 1996) are categorically phenomenal in the sense that they are open-minded and driven by love and care, some parents in this demographic can sometimes struggle with leadership and responsibility. At times, this generation wants harmony so much that they can find it difficult to say "no" to their children.

Millennials, due to numerous factors that occured while they were growing up, are characterized as a generational group that need praise to feel good. Knowing this, it's no surprise that many people in this age group crave positive reinforcement (smiles, giggles, calm) from their babies and use that as a barometer to measure if they are being "good" parents. Of course, not every person born during this time will feel this way, but research has shown that many people do—and it's not a bad thing! It's a product of the social environment in which this generation was raised.

While nothing but good intentions are behind this approach, parents need to be careful. Yes, everyone wants a happy baby, but babies can't be happy all the time—and that is okay! Happiness comes from learning all the emotions and being equipped to cope with them in relationships with others, as that's life.

Children learn fast and if a parent is always giving in, or quickly trying to make an unpleasant situation pleasant or unnecessarily easy for the baby, then the child may come to understand "my parents can not handle when I am unhappy." When this happens, a child can internalize emotions to a fault and then when a difficult feeling becomes too much for that child it results in feeling anxious or angry. This occurs because that child has not adequately learned about all feelings and has not learned the skills to cope with them.

Similar patterns can occur in a child that has parents who are not comfortable making tough decisions. In these scenarios, at times, the child takes on the role of the "adult" by becoming "the good child." This child may later suffer from anxiety and become fearful of disappointing her parents. This child can feel her parents anxiousness around decisions and may grow to become an anxious child, and adult, who has a hard time setting personal boundaries and making decisions herself, too. On the other hand, some children who live in this way may become very dominant and tend to be disrespectful. They take on the adult responsibility and become the boss who wants to dictate how situations go.

When parents understand that total harmony is an illusion in close relationships and can accept full adult responsibility, their children can rest and just "be kids." In a relationship between two adults we own 50% of the responsibility of the quality of the communication and relationship. In a relationship with a child the adult has 100% of the responsibility.

As you take on the leadership role, your baby's energy will go towards development, which is exactly where it should be focused. Your baby, with time, will respect you and know you love them and care for them, and that saying "No" sometimes is meant to protect and guide them towards growth or safety. They may not be able to fully understand, or vocalize the acknowledgment that you are taking care of them for years to come, but the foundation of the relationship is set.

When a parent can master saying "No" with empathy and an understanding of how to find the balance, the relationship is stronger for it. And happiness will prevail.

Chapter 3

"All your dreams can come true if you have
the courage to pursue them."
– Walt Disney

The Gift of Swim:
Give Your Child a Head Start

From a physical perspective, water stimulates us, it challenges us. It resists us even as it buoys us up. It allows us to move in graceful, new ways and helps develop our sense of balance. From an emotional perspective, water is special in the way that it can be fun and enriching while sometimes also seeming a little dangerous and unsure. Water is also alive! It moves, and the fluidity and dance of water in turn moves us. It responds to our touch and stimulates us, making water something extremely interesting for a child to explore.

Your baby will be naturally inclined to like water, because it reminds her of the warm, protected time in the womb where she did somersaults to heartbeats and got ready for life in the world.

Studies show that most children who start swimming activities early in life get a head start in development, not only physically (motor growth) but also socially and intellectually (cognitive growth).

The findings of the four-year project by the Griffith Institute for Educational Research, led by Australian Educational Researcher Robyn Jorgensen, recommended that *"all infants and children receive the opportunity to swim as a way to better themselves."* Her team concluded that *"swimmers exhibited multiple advantages and emphasized, among other things, that children who had participated in swimming were better prepared to start school."* The study went on to explain that intensive testing of children using internationally-recognized tests, confirmed that children who swam, from early in life, often performed significantly better than the normal population across many measures of physical, cognitive, social and linguistic measures.

It turns out that the difference between your child becoming a little dolphin, or instead, becoming water-averse, has less to do with the experience itself than with how, and why, she is in the water in the first place.

Do you love the water? Are you nervous yourself in the water? Are you a great swimmer, but nervous when you think about your little one in the water?

It can't be overstated how your feelings and actions, subconscious or conscious, can rub-off on your baby who looks to you for security, comfort and support during many moments of the day.

Your baby is born with all the basic emotions—he feels them, but doesn't understand them yet, as he is just a little person in the making! Your baby needs you to understand and regulate his emotions in the beginning, and with your support and guidance he will gradually learn to understand them and later to regulate them himself. With this in mind, it's important to be aware of your own emotions and respond to your child's emotions and feelings with an open mind.

What may seem mundane or uninteresting to an adult is absolutely fascinating to a baby who is seeing the world with fresh eyes. Almost everything they are seeing, hearing and experiencing is brand new. Give your baby the courtesy of being awestruck with him while he absorbs his surroundings, whether in the water while swimming or on land through various situations. Even an errand like going to the market for food can become a world of colors, smells and sounds, which is a huge learning opportunity for your child. You can help make it fun and exciting by engaging in the experience with him.

As it relates to swimming, if your baby is naturally an extrovert then she may be more open to new experiences, whereas an introvert reflects, absorbs and needs a little more time to warm up to a new situation. As the parent, watching facial and body cues will allow you to respond and offer reassurance and loving support, in real time. In a swim class, you'll quickly discover if your baby is an extrovert or introvert, which will help you respond accordingly in a variety of situations to help your child feel comfortable and learn in a way that is best for them.

Listen to your baby as she provides communication cues which will tell you what captures her interest, what she needs and what she wants. Is she splashing around, calm and happy? Or is she experiencing information overload and in need of your soothing support to remove her from a situation so she has time to process and relax? Not every baby will be happy the moment they enter the water. Rather it is through practicing the lessons that swim offers, together on an ongoing basis, that can lead to healthier, stronger relationships for both parent and baby.

Oliver's Story

I was teaching a group of parents with very young babies, only a few months old. This story is about two sets of students, Oliver and his Mom, and Lily and her Mom. The babies were quick to show curiosity towards the water and swimming from the instant they entered the pool area. Upon seeing the water, they immediately wanted to feel it and when their hands hit the surface—splash!—some water splattered up in their faces.

The splash caught Oliver's Mother by surprise and she immediately worried that it had frightened the child. She rushed to lift him out of the water and comfort him, as if he was frightened of the splash even though he didn't show any signs of unease. The scared feeling was her own, not her son's—she was the one who needed reassurance. He wasn't scared of the splash and despite his Mom's worried reaction, he kept reaching out toward the water, curious to interact with it and feel the warm water against his skin as he splashed again.

Even with Oliver clearly exhibiting signs of being curious and happy with the new experience, his Mom couldn't seem to relax. She held her baby close, in an uneasy cradle, smiling with uncertainty, clearly nerved by the experience.

Luckily for Oliver, his Mom was in my class where myself and other parents were able to help provide reassurance and ease her worries. Afterall, she was as much our student, as Oliver was since learning together means the parents are learning too.

Of course, parents want the best for their babies, so it was my job to assure her that Oliver was in great hands (her hands!) and that the water was nothing to be afraid of. She eventually relaxed and as I explained more about the importance of the parent and child interaction and how it can build confidence in the water. As she understood more, she carried an openness to allowing Oliver to explore in future classes. When Mom relaxed, Oliver could also relax, as he viewed his Mother as a source of assurance and guidance. If she stayed timid, he might also have become timid of swimming in general, and chances are he may not have enjoyed swimming even though his initial instinct around water was positive.

Learning to self-regulate emotions for a parent is very important on the overall experience, as parents are the leader and the baby looks to you to help them manifest emotions. This ties back to the micro-dynamics of the relationship, as parents can help their babies organize their thoughts and feelings, helping them to express those feelings. When a baby has a feeling that doesn't match their parents' response, it can confuse the baby as they try to process the emotions, and it can also send mixed messages to the baby's developing brain. In this case, even though Oliver was initially calm, if his Mom remained uncomfortable and nervous every time they swam, those emotions could imprint to Oliver and change his long term impression of the water and swimming. Luckily for everyone that did not happen and Oliver and his Mom went on to be beloved swimmers of mine who soaked in every experience the water brought their way. It built self-esteem, independence and a zest for life within both of them, while also strengthening the bond between them.

The overall lesson of this story is that Mom projected her own emotions onto Oliver and it made it difficult for her to see how her son felt. Oliver's own experience and feelings of splashing in the water didn't match his Mother's anxious response to the water "hitting his face." For a child who is learning about the world and developing his emotional understanding, upon seeing his Mom's reaction he might have wondered, "Will water hurt me?" or "Why is Mommy so upset?" His Mother's reaction could unknowingly cause confusion in Oliver and trigger anxiousness in him that would affect his experience in the water, and also perhaps carry on to make him more timid on land too.

Lily's Story

Now, Oliver's friend Lily was also splashed, getting water on her face, but her Mom responded differently. When the splash occurred, Lily was caught off guard and a little nervous about the water, but her Mom was emotionally grounded and calm, responding to her daughter's surprised reaction with great eye-contact, a reassuring smile and a happy attitude that reassured Lily she was safe. Lily could see, and feel, the good vibes from her Mom which gave her comfort and made the experience of splashing an enjoyable one. She tried to splash again and this time she wasn't nervous because she trusted her Mom and knew she was in great, safe hands. The water was fun! The trust between Lily and her Mom was already forming into a strong bond (as is the case with most primary caregivers and their baby), so Lily's Mom responding in this way made Lily think, "if my Mom likes splashing, and I wasn't hurt or bothered by the splash, then I can like splashing too!" There was no sense of harm, nerves or mixed feelings on how Lily should feel about the water splashing her. There was clearly nothing to worry about, which opened Lily up to bravely explore the water more. This initial interaction in the pool made all of Lily's experiences in the water better. Learning to swim, with interest and the security of knowing she was safe, with Mom by her side made all the difference.

New Way to Parent

We're in the midst of a paradigm shift from a style of parenting preoccupied with authority and correction, to one focused on connection and empathetic guiding. *Harvard University's Center on the Developing Child communicates that "safe, predictable, supportive and responsive relationships early in life are the most important factors for health, learning and in building sturdy brain architecture".*

Many people from previous generations were of the mindset that a baby should adapt to its surroundings. There was an emphasis placed on not "over coddling" babies for fear it would make them needy, or weak, and lead to negative outcomes. Methods such as the "cry it out" approach to sleep-training were developed. As it relates to swimming schools, many parents were taught to dunk their baby under the water in the first class. If the baby cried, teachers would instruct parents to continue to do it, as that is "how babies learn."

Learning cannot be accomplished well under stressful situations, so in fact this was doing no good for the babies, or the relationships between the babies and their parents, because trust was being lost. In general, advice was generic: a one-size fits all approach. There was a belief that "tough love" was the best way to approach parenting a baby, in order to raise a "strong" person who turned into an adult that could handle life. Parenting styles also differed from country to country, and each country thought their way was best.

Fast forward to today. The world is a smaller place, with mostly open-minded parents who welcome information from various cultures to find the right balance for their family. Many parents today accept that what works for one child may not work for another, and that it is important to invest the time to find out how to best parent to an individual baby.

Research has found that it is impossible to "over coddle" an infant under the age of one year. A baby is so primal, pure, honest and direct, that when a baby gives a parent a cue, it is their way of telling the parent what they need. "I'm hungry," "I need my diaper changed," "I love snuggling with you," "I'm tired and need to go to sleep." The more a parent spends time with their love bug, the more they come to understand the nuances of their individual child and what that child is communicating to them. In this way a parent can begin to learn how to best respond to the individual needs of the baby. As this happens, the relationship blossoms and the positive benefits begin to unfold.

It's also important for a parent to *accept* that parenting isn't always going to be easy even when you're doing everything "right." Experiencing ranges of emotions is human nature and key for a healthy individual. The journey and lessons that you learn with your baby, as a family, and how you cope with them, together, is what can bring growth for everyone and a joy that is unmatched!

Role reversal: View the world from your child's eyes and "tune-in"

Often, at the start of the baby swimming process, many parents find themselves preoccupied with their own feelings and doubts. Anxiety, insecurity or a feeling of being out of control can occur. Even parents who are enthusiastic about a swim program, and can't wait to try it with their baby, sometimes forget to tune-in to their child once the swim class gets going.

If you find yourself in this position, my message to you is that this is an excellent opportunity to work on your own self-control. You can do this by becoming aware and improving your response to your emotions in stressful situations. This will help you relax and become more present and aware of your child's experience and needs, and respond to your baby's needs better. The best place for your baby when he's in the water is in your loving arms, and when you are present it is easier to gently guide your baby through different motions. As you do this, keep an eye on your baby's reactions and cues, so that you are able to respond quickly and adjust as needed. This promotes teamwork.

When you get to swim class, or a private pool that has good conditions for a baby, you may be very excited and hopeful that your child will love the experience. Try not to put too much pressure on this. It's okay if your baby doesn't immediately light up and show signs of enthusiasm as he enters the water. If your baby isn't visibly enthusiastic, it doesn't necessarily mean he is unhappy. Some babies simply are more cautious and need time to absorb situations, while other babies are quick to react to a new situation with ease. Listen to your munchkin's cues and take the journey into the pool together. The relationship you will form is invaluable and the lessons you will learn will be beneficial in all areas of life.

"Tune-in" to Your Child

"Tuning-in" means recognizing and responding to your child. It's about doing your best to view the world through your baby's eyes and mind.

Consider how new everything is and the process your baby is going through while she absorbs the many stimuli around her. Every new sight, touch, sound, smell and taste that your baby experiences is fresh "content" for her to process.

Imagine yourself in that position. If it sounds exciting, a little nerve-wracking and exhausting, that's because it is. In fact, the reason babies sleep so much is because they are learning every moment they are awake. Each nap they take throughout the day (and night) ensures that their brains have time to process, field and store information to help them learn and remember as they grow.

It's incredible when you step back and consider that every single thing a baby sees, smells, hears, touches and does is completely new in the beginning. While they experience all the new senses, and all the emotions that come with this new information, nothing is sorted yet. By tuning-in, parents can help their babies understand, organize and become the best version of themselves, by giving individualized responses and guide their children through what all these new experiences mean.

How to Tune-in: To help you tune-in, consider thinking through the following process, which will help you not only view and understand a situation (in the water or otherwise), but also respond to your baby's needs in a way that is healthy, safe and enjoyable.

By following this guide, you can better assess and individualize a situation (keeping in mind that every baby and parent are different), which will make the overall experience better for you and your baby. Ultimately, this process will lead to an emotionally healthy and happy baby and a healthy, happy family dynamic!

- Gauge your own state of mind in the moment.
  - How do you feel? What are you excited or concerned about?
  - With awareness of your own emotions, you're ready to focus on those of your baby and not project yours onto him.
- Pretend you are your baby. Try to imagine what your baby may be thinking and feeling in the moment.
  - How would you feel if you were experiencing the situation for the first time? What would you need?
- Be sensitive to the newness of each and every detail of your baby's surroundings.
  - Think through the five senses—sight, touch, sound, smell and taste. How may these new sensory experiences may be impacting your little one? How many new people are around? How is the temperature in the pool or room? What does it smell like? How bright, or dark, is the light? What new sounds are your baby hearing?
- Be mindful that as the parent you are responsible to give your baby what she needs.
  - You are equipped to take note of your child's facial and body cues while also assessing the environment around you. If a situation is too overwhelming (for now), then make the world smaller and more manageable for your baby. You may also need to make the decision to leave. If your baby is ready for a situation (e.g., looks calm, relaxed, curious), then continue to explore together.
    - For example: When you enter the pool, if your baby is engaged and curious, join in and enjoy her exploration. If your baby starts crying and wants to stay close to you, respect her wishes and go slow. If the crying escalates, leave the water. This will ensure your baby knows you are tuned-in to her needs, while also showing love, affection and leadership.

By tuning-in, you will find a balance that comes from listening to your baby and will be able to provide a healthy, safe environment that is fun and enjoyable. It's an incredible way to help strengthen your relationship from the start, as tuning-in will help your baby build trust in you, and in herself. Your baby will notice that you are listening and being mindful of her needs as an individual, which is the building block for a strong emotional, and empathetic, person in the making!

Chapter 4

38

"I've learned that people will forget what you said,
people will forget what you did, but
people will never forget how you made them feel."
– Maya Angelou

Learning Together

Your baby is learning and growing each day. Everything is new. Some situations are easier than others, but with your help you'll get through it together.

It's important to remember that many of these experiences, now with a baby in the mix, are new for you too. Perhaps not in the same way, but they are new in the context of you leading as a parent and being responsible for this little being. That can be a lot of pressure and feel overwhelming at times for parents and caregivers.

Remember to go easy on yourself, be patient and take comfort in knowing that many people in your situation feel the same. It helps if you can be mindful to be present and to try to be your best self, while also understanding that you will make mistakes and need time to grow, too. In your baby's eyes you are already the best, so enjoy the journey of learning together.

Luca's Story

Luca, six months old, is making his first visit to the pool to try baby swimming with his parents. Everything he encounters at the pool is new—new sounds, new smells, many new people—and his sensory system is being overloaded. He presses closer to his Dad, who responds by making eye contact and speaking to him soothingly. Having Dad's calm voice as an anchor helps the child relax, while Mom is busy attending to the practical details of setting up his swimming gear and getting the family organized before entering the water. Luca seems to be okay, but as soon as Mom and Dad want to undress him, the little boy starts to cry...

The family has come to my swim school with plenty of time before class, which gives Dad time to pick Luca up again and try to soothe him. He cradles him and speaks to him quietly. The two sit for a moment, looking at the water and the other swimmers, and Dad notices Luca relaxing again. This time it's easy to take off his clothes, as he remains in his Father's lap with Mom also by his side. The family takes their time getting Luca dressed in his swimsuit and talking to him about what is going to happen while they are at the pool.

Once Luca is in his swimsuit, and appears to be comfortable, the family slips into the water and Luca stiffens once again. Dad continues to hold him close, which reassures him.

The swim lesson begins with a song—a familiar one Luca knows from bath time at home. He meets his Father's gaze and Dad smiles, both of them recognizing the familiar tune, as they sing along. Soon Luca is engaging in the water movements and following along with the rest of the class, smiling at Dad.

Dad is tuned-in to Luca, so knowing that his son gets tense easily, he adjusts his pace to move at a slower speed that keeps his boy calm, comfortable and able to follow along. When he sees Luca is still smiling, Dad gradually picks up the tempo and soon the baby is giggling, along with his Father, and is in pace with the rest of the students.

From Tub to Swimming Pool

Luca's parents had been looking forward to joining the swim class for a long time. Knowing that his time in the bathtub at home was one of the favorite parts of his day, Luca's parents researched to prepare well and just knew he would love the pool.

They are an inspiring set of parents. Each is very supportive of the other, and they are both eager to understand their son's needs and do their best to meet them.

Dad is generous with his love and is sensitive towards listening to Luca. His parents are mindful to help him feel safe, comfortable, stable and reassured in unfamiliar situations. Luca also longs for structure, context and an understanding that he can trust the situation he is in, which will come in time as he builds regularity and experience in a situation. For a baby, finding comfort and a feeling of safety, rhythm and movements can have a magical effect. In Luca's case, he went from feeling unsure about swimming, to enjoying it because his parent paid attention to his emotions and let him approach it at his own pace. It allowed Luca to relax in the new environment, and open himself up to the activities and experience of swimming with his parents.

The first time Luca and his Dad entered the pool, Dad was extra aware of the surroundings and thought through how his baby may be feeling. He's very fond of water himself and he hoped Luca would like swimming, too. During the first class, and each class thereafter, both parents made sure their son had their full attention and support, so that it was obvious to Luca and would help build up his confidence. The parents know how important they are to Luca; it's a cherished feeling to know your child depends on you so much, and with this love in mind, they wanted to give all that love back and then some. It was precisely because the emphasis had changed at my swimming lessons that this positive experience was possible. Parents understood that the primary focus was on nurturing each child's feelings rather than on the exercises. By focusing on the feelings first, the activities came naturally, once the baby was ready.

By enjoying swimming in this way, every child, including Luca and his parents, had a very happy experience where they learned and grew together.

Luca is a great example of how listening to your baby and "tuning-in" works wonders.

Sometimes, however, a parent needs more time to learn themselves. This was the case with Chloe and her mom. The following is their story.

Chloe's Story

Chloe and her Mom are equally nervous as they enter the pool. As they wade in to join the larger group, Mom's thoughts are spiraling with numerous worries, "Am I holding her properly? Do the other parents notice me fumbling around? What if Chloe doesn't like the water? Ugh, I hate a scene... will I get my money back if she hates to swim? I can't believe it took months to get into this class and now that we're here, I'm already regretting it!"

The nerves and stress started well before they entered the water.

They were late leaving the house, and as Chloe got buckled into her carseat, she started crying. "Please, not now Chloe," Mom pleaded to her daughter. Mom hurried to find a pacifier and when her little girl had settled down she rushed her into the car and off they drove to swim class.

Chloe was teething. She had missed her nap and wasn't feeling great. Mom was tired too, from tending to her little one throughout the night. They simply weren't having a great day and were both a little off, but because this was the first class and Mom had waited so long to get into it, she didn't want to look like they were "bad students" and not go. Plus, the swim class was a financial investment and Mom knew that swimming had worthwhile benefits for Chloe's well-being.

They arrived late at the pool, so Mom hurried to get herself ready and then quickly started to undress Chloe, who immediately began to cry. The faster Mom moved, the harder the little girl cried, which in turn only increased the stress Mom was feeling. Once Chloe was in her bathing suit, and wrapped in a towel, Chloe's Mom tried to soothe her by holding and rocking her, trying to feed her (even though she had just eaten), but nothing was working. As time went on, Chloe relaxed and Mom took that as a sign that she was ready to go into the water and join the class that had already started.

"This is so embarrassing," She thought to herself. Once in the pool, Chloe instantly started to cry again.

At this point, it's all becoming a little too much for Mom. "How did I end up with a child that cries all the time? This happens at home and now in the water too!?" She feels as if she's on the verge of giving up and crying herself.

As I mentioned earlier, all parents have the best intentions and the parents in my swim school were as much our students as the babies. In this case, Mom needed reassuring words, understanding and empathy. Once Mom relaxed, we knew it would become easier for her to help Chloe relax too. Mom appreciated the kind smiles and camaraderie. As she let go of her worries, so did her little girl. Chloe slowly became less tense and stopped crying.

Even though Chloe had relaxed, she was really worn out from having her limits pushed too far. Sometimes, after doing their best to determine why (in this case lack of sleep and teething) and follow their child's needs, parents might have to accept that their child is simply not having a good day. Chloe looked tired, so I advised her Mom to make Chloe's world "smaller" by moving to the corner of the pool where she could comfort her with no people and fewer noises. It was beneficial because it was less overwhelming to Chloe (and her mom).

This worked and Chloe was soon splashing the water with interest and curiosity, in the comfort of her Mother's arms. Chloe's Mom interpreted her daughter's interest to mean they should rejoin the class. Chloe was not ready for this and as soon as they entered the group, she began to cry again to her Mother's confusion. Why is this happening?

Mom's stress was affecting Chloe. Chloe's Mom means well of course, but isn't realizing that her angel needs not only her physical presence, but her emotional presence too. Mom is unconsciously more concerned about fitting in with the other moms than listening to Chloe's needs in this moment. If she was more in-tune with her daughter, she'd realize Chloe was too exhausted to take on this new experience today, and to instead try again during next week's class.

Mom's own stress to help Chloe have a great first swim class caused her daughter more stress. Mom loves her daughter very much, make no mistake about it, but in this situation she lacked the ability to offer her the comfort, leadership and security she needed. Chloe can sense her Mom is not in-tune with her and she is therefore communicating this to her Mom in the only way she can, which is through tears and body language that says "I feel overwhelmed and confused. I am not happy. I need you to see me!"

What Might Mom Have Done?

Chloe is a first born child. Being a first born means a lot of things. First-born children often receive undivided love and attention, but also have parents that are learning how to parent for the first time (and who may not always get it right, at first). The saying, "practice makes perfect" is true for everyone—babies and parents. In this case, Chloe's Mom is learning. As a new parent, Chloe's Mom is still learning to balance what she thinks is the right decision and what is actually the right decision based on her daughter's needs. She is learning how to tune-in to her peanut and once she is able to do this, she and her daughter will grow stronger together as a team. Right now, there is an unintentional disconnect and a struggle occuring. This is because Chloe's Mom is acting on what she thinks is best based on society standards, instead of reacting to her daughter's individual needs.

When a parent decides to have their baby take place in an activity, such as swim class, simply attending that activity with your child doesn't automatically fulfill the obligation of doing "your duty." You need to be fully present (with your whole heart), in the moment, to help your baby adjust, learn and grow. Babies learn and develop by trying new things, but a child who is feeling stress, like Chloe, is operating from the most primal portions of her brain and will have a hard time learning anything new. By contrast, when she feels safe and comfortable, the more complex regions of her brain are activated and the door to learning is opened.

Parents acknowledging their baby's emotions is extremely important. When empathy is shown, a baby can feel that their parent fully understands their feelings and is trying to help them, which in turn teaches a baby how to cope with those feelings. By tuning-in and working your best to keep your baby calm, your child will learn that the world is a wonderful place to be. Your child also learns that when he needs it, you will be there to help. In this way the solid foundation of trust is built.

Chloe's Mom wanted to be her best self for her daughter (as almost all parents do!), so as time went on she indeed became more aware and in control of her own emotions. This allowed her to better meet, help, sooth and regulate her daughters emotions, which blossomed their relationship.

Through the gift of swim, we were able to help coach Chloe's Mom in childhood relationships, as well as the act of swimming. While swimming, Mom and daughter began to understand and enjoy each other more, having fun on the journey of learning together while in the water. They created rituals that included arriving to class early to have pre-pool snuggle time and Chloe's Mom learned to respond to her daughter's mood in real-time, caring solely about Chloe and not what other people may think. The positive change this "dynamic duo" created in the water was even something they brought home to their daily life, which greatly impressed Dad, too. The house felt happier and calmer for everyone. This is a great example of how swimming together was the catalyst for strengthening the parent-child relationship, and leading to overall happiness.

You Are Not Alone

Are there times when you feel insecure as a parent? I know I sure did when my two children were younger! Especially in the beginning, and in new situations, the influx of change and newness in your life can feel overwhelming at times. In the meantime, the world teems with a mixture of cultures and overlapping generations that exhibit a broad range of approaches to parenting, which doesn't exactly make it any easier. Sure, comparison and recommendations can be useful and enriching, but also overwhelming when you aren't sure which advice is best to listen too. In the end, it's about finding what works best for your baby and your family.

I hope this book can support you in the water and get you swimming towards more awareness and clarity about what benefits *you*, *your* child and *your* relationship, while also learning about what doesn't work. In the end, it's not about right or wrong, it's about learning to be responsible for the quality of the relationship. When this is done, your child can experience the world as an interesting, good place where adults help in times of difficulty and need. This style of parenting is what will give your child a great start in life and also a deeper connection to you.

Chapter 5

"The best and most beautiful things
in the world cannot be seen or even touched.
They must be felt with the heart."
– Helen Keller

Finding Family Balance Through Secure Attachments

A secure attachment is vital in determining how a human relates to closeness, protection and care. It is also imperative as you consider the characteristics of independence, joy of discovery and trust in one's own strength and ability. It even provides a blueprint for future relationships.

More and more attention is now devoted to the importance of a safe attachment and to the serious consequences that can result from its absence.

Alan Sroufe, a Developmental Psychologist at the Institute for Child Development at the University of Minnesota, found that "nothing is more important than the 'attachment relationship.'" Over a 35-year period, the Minnesota Longitudinal Study of Risk and Adaptation revealed that the quality of the early attachment reverberated well into later childhood, adolescence and adulthood, even when temperament and social class were accounted for.

During my work with parents and children, it became clear that the quality of the relationship had a great impact on a child's behavior and how well they shared in activities together. It was also clear that it had an effect on the parents feelings towards parenthood. Good relationships fostered a feeling of joy and happiness!

Secure attachments impart a feeling of being loved. Each of us needs to feel we have value as a human being and we belong. In fact, it is such a vital need, that the United Nations has identified it as a basic human right. The U.N. Convention on the Rights of the Child states that it is an adults' responsibility to do what is best for children and to consider how children are affected by an adult's decisions.

Being loved—just for being YOU—means everything to your child's ability to learn and develop.

A Healthy Bond Is a Joint Effort

Attachment is a cooperative venture. The better the connection between the parents, and between the parents and child, the greater the individual's, and family's, well-being will be. This also leads to a more conducive environment in developing emotional intelligence that will impact other areas of growth.

When family bonds exude security and trust, the child learns by experience that her parents are responsive to her needs, accepting and supportive. In return, the child is more likely to be joyful and happy to explore her world! When your love bug is happy, you are happier too and the cycle of happiness develops confidence and a stronger family unit. While parents take responsibility for the overall quality of the family dynamic, all family members—including the child—are imperative to building a happy, trusted bond that feels secure.

It's important to also understand that as a parent, a lot of energy is exerted on a daily basis, and you need to feel supported too! When a parent feels support from a trusted, secure network of people (family or friends) it can greatly help the parents ability to raise children in a happy home. The old saying that "it takes a village to raise a child" really is true, and I encourage parents not to shy away from asking for help when they need it.

Henry's Story

Ten-month-old Henry is in a cheerful mood when he and his Mom arrive at the pool and she prepares him for swimming. Dad is on his way to the pool to join them following his day at work. On his way over, Dad is thinking about how this is his activity and a great way to spend quality time with his little boy. But once Dad arrives, Henry's happy disposition changes...

Dad arrives soon after Mom and son are ready. The child is happy to be there. "How's it going today?" Dad asks. Last time, things didn't go so well as Henry cried the entire lesson.

Sure enough, when the child realizes he's about to be separated from his Mom, he immediately looks away from his Dad and clings to her. Mom tries handing him over, reassuring him everything is okay, but Henry grasps onto her, unsure and not ready for his "safety zone" to be taken from him. To him, his Mom is his whole world! Eventually Dad manages to pry him loose, but as the two of them make their way into the water, Henry just cries and looks for Mom, reaching his arms out to her.

Not surprisingly, this is upsetting to Dad. "What's wrong with me?" he might be wonde-ring. "Why doesn't Henry like me? Am I really up to being a Father?"

Henry's Father is an executive at a large company that requires many hours at the office or away on business. While he is busy, he prioritizes the family's swim classes in order to bring him together with his son for a special weekly bonding session. As good as Dad's intentions are, Henry isn't sharing the same enthusiasm. Dad starts wondering if continuing the swim classes are even worth it. He's beginning to think, "If this is the way things are going to be, what good does setting aside this quality time do?"

Because Dad works a lot, and also travels frequently, he doesn't have a standard routine at home the way his wife does. For Henry, there is no routine or natural rhythm with Dad. Instead it's his Mother who is the ever-present, primary attachment and therefore Mom is the person he relies on and wants to be around. When they now get to swim class and Dad takes Henry away from his Mom, Henry gets upset.

Henry is experiencing classic separation anxiety.

Separation Anxiety

Separation anxiety is a developmental stage. It represents the stage of development at which time a child begins to show a clear preference for a primary caregiver and gets upset when they are separated from that person. The feeling for the baby is new and can often be strong in the beginning, but with your help the baby will learn how to handle the separation and understand that it is only short-term. For example, your baby learns that if you leave the room during a nap, or leave the house all together, you come back to reunite. The skill of learning how to cope with separation anxiety needs to develop and is something some adults may take for granted, or find difficult, to fully understand.

It can be scary for your baby to be in your safe arms watching your smiling face one minute, and the next minute—*poof!* your baby finds himself separated from you, as if you have vanished! What a cruel magic trick. With all of this in mind, I urge you to be kind and mindful of how your baby may be feeling so that you can help him cope and learn how to manage this new feeling.

Back to Henry's Story....

Put yourself in Henry's shoes. Try to picture things as they look to him and you'll see why it might be unnerving.

From his perspective, he is *part* of Mom, *one with* her... and all of a sudden it seems like she is leaving and he is being taken from her. His awareness is growing and this ignites new feelings of separation and causes anxiety. That's a scary feeling for Henry. He may be thinking, "what if Mom doesn't come back? How will I cope without her?? I need my Mom!"

Essentially, a secure attachment is about a circle of trust. A child can have secure attachments with both parents, siblings, a nanny, grandparents, aunts, uncles, etc., yet there is most often a hierarchy. There will be that one person, in the first few years of a baby's life, that the child seeks first if he or she is there. A wider circle of people who loves and cares for your little one, is a win-win, as the more love your baby receives, and is able to give, the healthier everyone will be emotionally.

Dad is a little uneasy that Henry doesn't want to go to him, stinging from feelings of rejection and insecurity. He isn't sure whether Henry wants to be in the water with him as much as he wants to be in the water with Henry.

Mom is tuned-in to Henry, and her husband, and knows that she can help them figure out how to find comfort in this situation. She also understands how meaningful this time is for Dad to have with his son.

Mom helps by getting into the water and showing Henry her happy, loving feelings towards Dad, while they all play together. By joining them in the water, Mom, Dad and Henry are a trio—a team! Mom holds Henry to calm his nerves, reassuring him that she is present, but is also interacting with Dad in a fun way. This shows Henry that Mom thinks Dad is great and that she trusts him, which in turn helps Henry feel that safe connection too. Mom and Dad are acting as partners in this scenario and it is extremely helpful for Henry to absorb. Babies are intelligent and this is a cue for Henry.

As Henry comes to understand that he won't be forced to be separated from Mom, he begins to relax. Dad stays present and active (encouraged by his wife), and the three of them continue to play together in an unrushed, loving, gentle way.

Dad plays games, such as peekaboo and diving down to blow bubbles to Henry's delight, while Mom smiles and laughs with her boys. The three of them, together, are having fun, and Dad and Henry are soon smiling wide at each other in full enjoyment.

Soon, Henry even reaches out for his Father which is a welcomed change and one that makes both Dad, and Mom, proud. At first the desire for Dad's arms is short-lived, but after a few swim classes where the parents focused on being a family unit in the water, showing Henry they were all a team, the baby began to enjoy being with his Dad as much as his Mom. Once the separation anxiety subsided, Mom bowed out gracefully to let Henry and Dad have their special time together, while she sat on the edge of the pool supporting their bond.

The importance of Mom and Dad supporting each other—not just supporting the baby—is key to opening up your baby's world of trust to a wider group of loving, trusting people in his life beyond the primary attachment person.

What You Can Do to Support a Safe Attachment

A parent's job is to understand, respond and regulate their baby's feelings, while giving the baby possibilities for exploring her world.

When we think about attachment to a primary caregiver, it is all around that person's ability to offer the child a sense of safety, security and love. A safe attachment offers a secure base for exploring the immediate surroundings, because the baby knows they have a trusted person standing by to provide protection from being overwhelmed and they also have you to help them feel safe while they enjoy their surroundings. That person also helps with regulating emotions by steadying the child when they're uneasy, and helping to elicit joy by finding experiences that bring forth happiness. By doing this, the primary caregiver helps their baby's emotional development so that she can gradually learn to understand her emotions and later learn to regulate them.

The parent (or other caregiver) that forms the secure attachment bond is predictable, dependable and responsive. Even with these great qualities, they are by no means perfect and shouldn't expect that of themself. This person has a deep love for the child and the child feels that love. This person is also a role-model for the child, guiding the child in social and cultural situations, doing their best to show the baby how to navigate the world. When a child has this person in her life, she'll grow to be a strong, self-sufficient, empathetic and happy adult.

In the absence of a secure attachment, a child is more likely to become insecure and exploration is impeded. This happens because it becomes not only hard for a baby to understand, and later learn to regulate their own emotions, but may also be harder for the baby to develop empathy towards themselves and others.

I encourage you to use the water to respond and engage in learning together with your baby. When something is a little challenging or scary, face it together! When something is fun and ignites feelings of happiness, be happy together! Empathy will help lead to secure attachments that will ensure happy babies and parents (or caregivers).

Emotional Workout for Babies: Peekaboo!!

A baby always takes an active part in their learning and development and one of the best ways to encourage this is through play. An example of this can be found when separation anxiety first awakens, which may be within the baby's first year. At that point most children and parents start to play peekaboo together—it's a universal game, loved by families in countries around the world. Not only is it a fun game for babies, it is also wonderful for cognitive development.

Peekaboo makes play out of the idea behind the child's greatest fear: being separated. In the game, the child repeatedly experiences the joy of seeing the familiar face of their loved one appear, disappear and reappear again. This ingenious emotional workout helps a baby understand, and eventually learn, how to handle the experience of separation by learning that the person will always come back. This helps your child begin to understand that the person is present, even when there is a level of separation involved.

Learning Through Attachment

More and more attention is now devoted to the importance of a safe attachment and to the serious consequences that can result from its absence.

In 2014, the Sutton Trust funded and published an American study that found that "Four in 10 infants lack strong parental attachments that are crucial to success later in life. These children are more likely to face educational and behavioral problems."

Attachment is vital in determining how a human relates to closeness, protection and care. It is also imperative as you consider the characteristics of independence, joy of discovery, and trust in one's own strength and abilities. It even provides a blueprint for future relationships.

Leading experts agree that practicing safe attachments needs to become common practice in households, institutions and learning environments around the globe. The reason is that safe attachments have a big influence on health, development and learning. When a baby has a strong attachment to someone, they pay attention to what that person is doing, which promotes better learning. When that person, in turn, recognizes the baby's ability to learn, and works with the baby to practice and absorb information, they are better able to learn problem solving skills and how to deal with failures and wins. It's no surprise when you think about the social and emotional creatures humans are, that we seek knowledge from, listen to and learn more from those we trust.

As it relates to swimming with babies to create safe attachments, there are many wonderful ways to promote this state of mind for your little one. Swimming is a natural activity, with a plethora of situations that support finding security that may build secure attachments between you and your baby. Swim is also a cross generational activity that bridges the age gap which allows people of all ages—beyond the parents—to bond with a baby in the water. That said, the most important aspect of baby swimming is always the relationship between you and your child, as you develop deeper bonds that will last a lifetime, because of the strong, quality attachment that being in the water can cultivate.

When the little child feels safe, he can relax and direct his full attention towards growth and development. During my years of teaching swim, I've seen over and over again how the wonders of the water help make it possible for a parent (or caregiver) and child to form a strong attachment bond. Through swimming together, lessons of being responsive, steady and dependable are present every time you enter the water, which makes it a great arena for learning.

Nothing Is Quite Like the Water

Being in the water is something you can do right from the newborn age. It allows you to move, interact and engage in ways you aren't able to do on land until months later. While you are connecting, you and your baby have the chance to fully immerse into the joy of swimming, together, as you learn and grow a stronger relationship with each other.

The water is a completely unique experience that can support building strong, safe attachments in many ways. Perhaps the most important difference that can occur by being in the water is the fact that you are eye-level with your baby. Rarely is this true in everyday life and while this may sound simple, being able to see eye to eye brings a closeness and equality to the relationship.

In the water there are also plenty of opportunities for skin to skin contact. Research has shown that bonding is critical in the early stages of a newborn's life. The act of "skin to skin" is practiced almost immediately upon a baby being born in most cultures around the world, because of the powerful bonding effect it can have. The skin to skin contact releases a love-hormone that also evokes calming neurobehavioral cues that fulfill basic biological needs for a newborn. In other words, it is extremely beneficial for a babies' (and parents') emotions, plus it supports healthy mental and physical health, by providing a sense of balance.

When swimming with your baby, there are many wonderful ways to promote bonding which leads to a secure attachment. According to child development experts, a secure attachment has at least three functions. I've used this research and applied it to swimming, so that you can practice secure attachments.

1. Provide a sense of safety and security by being predictable, present and responsive to your baby in the water.

2. Help your baby develop emotionally, by creating the best environment for learning. This means creating a space that is joyful and calm through various activities including motion, songs and interaction. It also means avoiding too many stimulants and to soothe your baby if she is feeling distress.

3. Be your baby's secure base and give her opportunities to explore and move in the water, which will help your baby develop and grow. After she has been exploring, be the safe harbour she can return to and relax with, before your baby's curiosity pulls her out again.

During the time you share with your baby in the water, you should practice finding balance between providing security and giving room for freedom and exploration to learn the many lessons. These lessons will be used in the pool and also on land to build trust, confidence, the foundation for resilience, secure attachments and so much more.

55

Chapter 6

56

"A bird sitting on a tree is never afraid of the branch
breaking, because its trust is not on the branch
but in its own wings. Always believe in yourself."
– Unknown

Growing From
Dependent To Independent

There is a tendency in today's society to encourage children to be independent as soon as possible. The fact is that humans have a hunger for relationships and deep connections. Children, in particular, develop their independence best, gradually, when they can depend on caring people and know they have a "safe haven" to retreat to when needed. In the relationship between you and your baby, your baby will learn and develop social cues, values and rules about the culture they live in.

When babies are born there is an inherent ability to connect and to form attachment to their parents. Knowing this, it's no surprise that from birth, a baby depends on his parents, or other primary caregiver. His most primal needs include your help providing food, warmth and safety. That dependency will be a key part of his life, especially in the first years as he is learning. Gradually, with your helping guiding him, your baby will reach for independence. This will come in time, when he is ready, and with your support you will help your baby build self-esteem, confidence and balance from within.

The Minnesota Longitudinal Study of Risk and Adaptation, mentioned in the last chapter, also found that "a secure attachment early in life led to greater independence later, whereas an insecure attachment led to a child being more dependent later in life. Independence blooms naturally out of a secure attachment."

You'll notice your baby's desire for independence slowly. For example, one day he may reach for the spoon while you are feeding him (wanting to maneuver the spoon himself), or he will take his socks off (which is much easier than putting them on!). In the water, he may try to reach for a toy or attempt to climb out of the pool wall and onto the deck. When you acknowledge and value your baby's initiative, and give your baby the opportunity to try and the time to practice, you are sending a clear message. You are saying through your actions, "I believe you can learn this, you are capable of it." These messages build a child's self-esteem and help children develop an inherent belief, from within, that says "I can learn!"

In contrast, if you notice your baby starting to take steps towards independence, but when he is not doing something correctly and you jump in to do it for him, it can send the wrong message. By taking over, you may mean well, but when this happens a message of "you can't do this" may accidently be sent, even though you are trying to help.

My recommendation is to tune-in and show support and guidance, while letting your little one explore. If he wants to try feeding himself, have an extra spoon ready, or take turns between feeding him directly and letting him attempt to feed himself. Support your baby's journey towards independence with your arms open for support and rest while instilling self-esteem, trust and balance from within.

By parenting in this way, you will foster independence in a caring and sensitive manner. Today, even science has learned and confirms that warm, sensitive care does not create dependency; it liberates and enables autonomy because children were always meant to learn from those they know and feel safe with. This style of parenting is how a child best learns to grow from dependent to independent.

Building Independence Through Swim

Swim offers an incredible vehicle to build trust and gradually, with good support, grow into independence. Independence is a stepping stone towards growth in other areas like self-esteem and self-confidence. The stronger the trust is between the baby and primary caregiver, the more independent your baby will likely become as she explores freely (knowing you are there to depend on, if needed). She will be happier, knowing she is loved and supported, but she'll also enjoy her freedom because she knows she is capable of doing things on her own.

While building these traits may be happening on land, swim is a perfect place to hone in on these life skills and uplevel an array of developmental areas for growth.

In the water, gravity is almost completely gone and the feeling of buoyancy and gliding is a treat for little ones and parents to enjoy! This new experience comes with new challenges. You and your baby may have a level of uncertainty, as you try swimming together for the first time, and your baby will likely depend on you to help show her the new environment. As you explore, you learn more about the water and about each other. As you practice swimming, and tuning-in, the joy and happiness you will find in the process will continue to grow.

New skills will also develop, as swimming positions are different than what your child is used to doing on solid ground. This includes motor, sensory, cognitive and emotional skill development. Swimming awakens senses, such as touch (tactile), balance (vestibular) and muscles and tendons (proprioceptive), which brings forth feelings that she wants to discover with you. Babies want to move freely in the water and as they move, they learn about buoyancy and the feeling of resistance. This resistance promotes muscle strength and motor development.

Babies that are introduced to water at a very early age (from 0-3 months) often swim in a style they create for themselves before they can crawl. At one-year old, that child may be able to do a whole series of swim "tricks" such as swimming short distances, turning around in the pool, jumping in and climbing out, all independently, with you by her side. That may not sound like much, but when you think about the nuances involved in infant/childhood development to reach these milestones, you come to understand it is something everyone in the family should feel great about.

It's the baby "swim strokes" towards becoming more independent.

59

Michael's Story

Little Michael, 10-months, and his Mother are playing by the pool wall. Michael wants to climb out of the pool, back on deck, so he can plunge back into the water, jumping into his Mother's arms. This is easier said than done.

He tries different angles and positions, but nothing works. Watching him, Mom has the urge to help, especially when he starts to register his frustration audibly, but she resists the temptation and finally her hunch pays off: he figures out the right combination of maneuvers and Michael manages to hoist himself up and out, onto the edge of the pool.

And what's the first thing he does once he has made it? He looks right at Mom to gauge her reaction. He wants to share his accomplishment with her! He thinks, "Did she see?? Did she see? I did it!" Oh, she saw. As their eyes meet in a proud moment for both Mom and son, it's smiles all around and celebratory expressions of delight.

Beginning when Michael was an infant, long before he could speak, the family developed a common "language" rooted in the baby swimming process. His parents learned how to tune-in to his signals and understand what he needed. That allowed him to express his feelings and make more sense of the world. When he was anxious or scared, they reassured him; when he was tired, they let him rest; and when everything got a little too much for him, they gave him their calming support.

Throughout it all, they trusted in the process of trying and learning, even with its frustrations. They shared his joy and made certain there was plenty of time for play and happy moments. In short, Michael's parents gave him a safe base from which to explore the world.

How Michael and His Parents Learned

To get him started, it was up to Mom and Dad to learn the framework. That began with simply spending time in the water with Michael. Just doing that, over time, taught them a lot about his needs and personality. In the water they were all at the same level, and the usual distractions, like cell phones and daily chores, were absent. They were free to focus on each other and the activity of swimming.

Mutual trust flourished and Michael knew he was in good hands. When he needed something, his parents helped; when he laughed, they laughed with him. He learned to trust and accept his feelings, even when they weren't so pleasant: disappointment, frustration, anger or fear. He learned that there was help and support if he needed it. The most important lesson he learned was that *his parents loved him for who he was and not for what he could do*. It didn't matter what milestones he achieved in the pool for the sake of achieving them, rather it was about being together and learning trust and balance as a family. Through swimming, he learned that many things in the world are fun to explore and that he could learn along with his parents.

A Parent Is a Leader

Children are creatures of "the now." Their frontal cortex has not developed fully, so they do not understand consequence and risk. They need their parents, or caregivers, to help guide them and ensure they are safe and cared for in the best way.

Michael's parents understood their responsibilities and their role of providing him with this guidance. They chose a pool and swimming school they liked, and a time of day they hoped would work best for his sleep schedule. After all, as we learned, sleep is key for mental balance, healthy growth and learning!

As leaders, they followed simple but important "rules" for family swim.

SAFETY: When he was in and around the water, they took full responsibility for his safety. They took safety precautions even after he had learned to swim, always being careful to ensure he felt he was in the best care.

ACCEPTANCE: Of course, there were days when Michael just wasn't in the mood for swimming. On such days, his parents could prepare all they wanted, but any attempt to force the issue only ended up with Michael crying. At those times, his parents might have felt their *own* feelings of frustration or irritation, but they learned that this was about Michael's integrity and respected it. His parents learning, and respecting, his boundaries was important if Michael was to learn to accept and respect boundaries for himself and others.

RESPONSIBILITY: The bottom line was that Michael's parents understood that it was their responsibility—from home, to the pool and back home again. It was up to his parents to make sure he was safe and happy, always.

As their swim teacher, I watched as they embraced that role and rejoiced in seeing them become more empathetic, flexible, caring and proactive towards Michael, during each class. His parents became pros at recognizing what they needed as a family—not only what Michael needed, but also how they worked best together to thrive and develop their emotional intelligence, together.

GUIDANCE: Babies don't have a concept of time or understand social and cultural rules. So in situations, like attending a swim class, rules are created for structure and the safety of everyone.

Excellent examples of structure to look for at quality swim schools include start and end times for swim classes, and free-play times available for families to participate in. In Michael's case, and for most babies, the structure and consistency gave him a sense of predictability and rhythm which helped release more energy for learning.

In the joined social activities, his parents developed an understanding in how they could direct and help him maintain focus, important core skills for life, from an early age. He also learned to handle difficult emotions, for example, Michael loved the water so he didn't always feel ready to come out of the pool when class was over. His parents accepted and acknowledged his feeling of disappointment and frustration, but acted as good role-models by following the rules and explaining to Michael why it was important to respect the rules. This made it easier for Michael to eventually learn how to accept the end of class, as he began to understand it was over, but that he'd be back again in a week.

The structure and rules helped Michael and his family become stronger together. They were dependant on each other, while also finding independence throughout swimming, which were skills that they could apply on land, too.

Overall, it's important to address feelings of a family unit, to promote healthy relationships. When you focus on supporting development in the beginning of a child's life, it's much better for their mental health, as it's easier to grow healthy children than to repair a broken adult. The feeling of being understood and being able to navigate the world better, fosters independence and leads to confidence, self-esteem (self-worth) and happiness at every age.

Chapter 7

"The whole world is a series of miracles,
but we're so used to
them we call them ordinary things."
– Hans Christian Andersen

Trust:
A Child's-Eye View

Trust is a feeling that exudes a sense of comfort and safety—both physical and emotional safety. This feeling is essential in building healthy relationships that lead to happy babies, who will become happy adults. While the concept of trust sounds simple enough, many struggle with it for a variety of reasons.

Building trust begins at birth when babies experience that their parents are responsive and indeed reliable. Over time, a strong bond of trust begins to form. With mutual trust, you will watch your child open up more and begin to show her personality in ways that are simply magical!

Sometimes trust is broken and needs to be repaired. A child who experiences caregivers that take responsibility of repairing trust when it is broken, will learn to trust again and take that ability into her adult life and future relationships.

Ella's Story

Ella is a one-year-old, who has been swimming with her parents since she was just a few months old. She is a happy little baby that loves her parents and trusts them very much. Her Mother and Father are self-aware people, who recognize they are developing their own skills as parents, as much as their daughter is learning more about herself in relationship to others. Together, this family is a unit that is on a journey of self-discovery and family happiness.

While Ella likes to be in the water, an issue keeps arising. Dad tends to get over-zealous with what he considers to be the fun aspects of swimming—things that he is nostalgic about from childhood. He has great intentions, but Ella doesn't understand the nostalgia behind Dad's excitement of certain activities, and Ella doesn't always share the same enthusiasm for what he wants to do. Unfortunately, Dad is having a hard time accepting this and rather than stay engaged and tuned-in to what Ella is already enjoying, he tries to push her towards other activities that he is "sure" will be even "more fun" for her, but Ella does not agree.

Mom knows that Ella will be happier focused on what she finds naturally enjoyable, but she stays quiet to avoid confrontation with her husband. She knows he means well and is nervous to hurt his feelings or stifle his enthusiasm.

This pattern continued over the course of a month, and each swim class Ella became less and less enthusiastic about the pool and swimming. Ella communicated as best as she could to express that she wasn't interested in certain activities her Dad found exciting. She'd make sounds to express she wasn't happy (sometimes crying, sometimes grunting) and her body language would clearly show when she did not want to do something (turning away).

Eventually, swimming became anything but fun for Ella. This had a lot to do with the family not being in sync, and because Ella could not explain her feelings and frustrations by talking, and because Mom was suppressing her own voice to explain to Dad what she saw happening, nothing was being resolved. This led to a frustrating dynamic for everyone. Her parents had good intentions, yet weren't able to have the foresight to see the larger issue developing, which was Ella forming a lack of trust in them, and a lack of trust in the situation.

Sliding Out of Trust

The "miscommunication" became clearer and came to a turning point on a day at the pool like many others. Everyone was in good spirits, and Mom and Dad wanted to introduce Ella to the slide. This did not go accordingly to their plan and the trust was officially lost at the pool.

Mom lifted Ella to the top of the slide, while Dad waited at the bottom to catch her. Her parents were so excited, sure that Ella would love it, but the slide was new to the child and she was a bit anxious. When her body got rigid, both parents noticed, but they didn't know what to do about it. Dad clearly remembered enjoying slides from his own childhood and honestly thought that once Ella experienced it for herself, she'd be saying "weeee!" down the slide herself.

Mom was with Ella at the top of the slide. Ella clung to her and tried to twist away from the slide to go back down to the landing—she did not want to try it. Mom sensed that Ella wasn't ready, but in an effort to appease her husband, she gave her a gentle push and down Ella went, slipping quickly on the slide and into the water. Dad was all smiles in the pool as he caught her at the bottom of the slide, but as he lifted the little girl out of the water, she started to cry. He comforted her as best he could, but she clung anxiously to him until the family left the pool for the day. At this point, she just wanted to go home.

Forget Yourself—Look at the Child

There's no question that Ella has a loving Father, who wants his daughter to have not only all the fun he had as a kid, but all the fun he *didn't* have. He wants her life to be even better than his own, something many parents strive to give their children.

Saying that, there's a fine line in parenting to ensure what you want for your baby is in their best interest and not your own. Sometimes the focus can turn in the wrong direction, as the adult's ego casts a shadow over the child's actual wishes and needs.

Often, parents of toddler aged children are most susceptible to these types of exchanges. When a parents' good intentions are rejected or fail, it can sting and may lead to doubt in one's mind, making them question if they are being a good parent.

Remember to Tune-In

During times that you feel unsure if what you are doing is best for your baby, my advice for you is to tune-in to their feelings, and do what you can to see the world through your baby's eyes.

By keeping a connection and remembering that the parent-child relationship is a two-way "dialogue," where you are responsible for the quality and reliability in the relationship, you will sooner be able to restore the good faith and trust in the child and relationship.

As a parent, you should expect and be open to an array of responses from your child. Stay curious, interested and engaged. Be patient and kind towards your baby—she is learning who she is, as much as you are. My advice to you is to enjoy watching how your little one navigates the world and notice the difference of opinions in situations. If your baby is curious and has the courage to try something directly—let her do it versus instantly trying to help her. Children need time to practice *how* to learn. They also need to make mistakes to build up confidence in problem solving, so that when they fail it's okay and they know they can simply try again...and eventually succeed.

We must also respect the fact that sometimes children need time to build courage. And for those babies that are a little more cautious, it's important to respect that characteristic and not push them to be how you think they should be. If you catch yourself doing this, simply make a mental note of it and try to do better yourself the next time. The better you can practice this, daily, the healthier the outcome will be to maintain—or restore—balance and trust. That's what responsibility in a loving relationship is all about.

Back to Ella's Story...

In talking with Ella's parents about how they felt things were going, they acknowledged that even though their intentions were good, the experience with the slide was not what they wanted for their little girl. Their child was left upset and they noticed her trust had been shaken. We talked through the importance of working to repair that trust to ensure her experience of swimming with them wasn't tarnished in the long-run, and more importantly, that trust was rebuilt as the parent-child bond is critical in all aspects of life.

Dad admitted that he may have been a little too enthusiastic and "pushy" towards his wants, and both parents agreed that it didn't feel good to force Ella into something she clearly wasn't ready for. Like most parents in this situation, they had no idea going down the slide—before Ella was ready—could have such a negative impact on the family relationship and Ella's happiness. To them, it was a simple, fun activity and nothing deeper. That said, it's extremely important to recognize, and acknowledge, that it was a deep experience for Ella, and also a negative one.

How to (Re)Create Trust

When trust is lost with a baby, building it back is extremely important and also fairly easy to do, when handled correctly.

In Ella's parents situation simply recognizing and accepting the issue was a step forward in finding a solution. After our talk I saw two parents who felt more secure in their parenting and their ability to communicate better as a family. Ella's parents realized that empathy and care must prevail, and that fear is overcome with understanding, a playful approach, and respect for the child's feelings rather than pressure. There was no doubt that Ella forgave her parents—that's what children do. Once a child has proof of their parents' responsiveness, trust is restored.

In time, the family was able to enjoy their sessions at the pool in a whole new way. Mom and Dad took responsibility for what had gone wrong, and restored peace of mind to the relationship, which in turn reinforced Ella's sense of trust. This process helped Ella develop confidence in herself, her parents, and eventually other people, which laid the groundwork for coping with life's challenges later on, making her more resilient and capable to face aversion.

Mistakes Are Valuable Opportunities

All people make mistakes—it's part of being human. Mistakes present valuable opportunities to learn, so it's not really about the accidents that happen and the mistakes you make, rather it's about how you handle those situations. When people take responsibility for their mistakes, and focus on how to repair any damage they may have done, the person is better suited to learn from their mistakes to improve in the future. It's about trial, error and growth!

Seeing how we cope with mistakes often becomes a "teaching moment" for our children, and a mistake handled in a healthy way becomes a lesson that promotes children's development and is a template they can use in their own relationships. The child learns that mistakes are part of life and that they can be corrected once a person learns what to do.

Ella and her parents were able to restore their trust, and Mom and Dad learned to talk through an uncomfortable situation honestly, without blame and conflict. It created a stronger partnership for them as a couple and the entire family had a closer bond from the experience.

Let's Try This Again...

On their next visits to the swimming pool, the family played close to the slide. Dad was holding Ella in the pool, and Mom slid toys and beach balls down it for them to catch. Ella and Dad watched in delight as toys came down towards them. Ella also recognized her fellow classmates going down the slide, with their parents close by, and saw the happiness they found from the experience. It didn't take long for Ella to start associating the slide as a fun place, too.

While the shift wasn't immediate, a few weeks later Ella got the urge to try the slide again. With a little help from her Mom, she made her way to the top. Upon standing up there, Ella changed her mind. "Nope, not ready," she said with her body language. Mom responded by nodding and picking her up into her arms, reassuring her that it was no big deal and they would try again another time. She took Ella into the pool to keep playing

with Dad, ensuring swim time was still on and very much fun. Mom and Dad were tuned-in and respecting Ella's wishes which made her feel happy and secure.

Upon being back in the water, Ella wanted to watch the slide and the other children going down it. She wanted to try again, but once at the top she'd change her mind, so they'd all go back into the water. This repetition went on, again and again. This is another example of micro-dynamics coming into play. Once Ella felt that her parents were on "her side" and saw her perspective, she didn't feel pressure and instead found interest in the slide herself, because she knew her parent's were there to protect her, help her and support her on this journey.

Finally, Ella found her courage. In her own time she decided when to try the slide and the result was pure joy and happiness! She loved it. This was a huge accomplishment for everyone in the family, as they worked together, as a team, to get to this point. Once Ella conquered her fear going down the slide, it became one of her favorite pool activities, which made her Dad very happy.

The lesson here is that Dad may have been "right" that his daughter ultimately loved the slide, but the steps to get there were different than his own experience. Listening to your child and tuning-in is what ensures a quality relationship that is lasting and built around trust, and that is the most important outcome of this story.

Your arms, your eyes, your voice and your actions are all channels for communicating playfulness, a sense of warmth and trust. A child who trusts you, will either share in your enthusiasm to try new things with you, or seek your support when a situation is too hard. Thanks to your great example, throughout life, your child will grow up to be a great person that is comfortable leading by example. For your part, seeing the world through your child's eyes opens up endless possibilities for bonding and a healthy, strong relationship for the rest of your lives.

Chapter 8

"There can be no keener revelation
of a society's soul than
the way in which it treats its children."
– Nelson Mandela

Respecting Your Child's Integrity & Finding Equal Dignity

A child's integrity is their pure state of being, as well as their physical and mental existence. It is who they are—pure, honest and true. Babies do not have the ability to be dishonest and they unapologetically tell it like it is.

That said, babies live in a world where adults are dictating most of their daily activities. It's easy for parents to overlook that their babies are needing to cooperate with many different situations throughout the day that may not be on the baby's terms at all.

In fact, babies are quite flexible and cooperative at adapting to most cultural and social situations. For parents, the important point is that you can acknowledge and see the world from the perspective of your baby. By doing this you are showing your child that she has, and that you respect, her integrity. This leads to a much healthier relationship because the baby will feel happy they are being "heard."

Equal dignity values the thoughts, feelings, needs and wishes of everyone in the room—baby or adult. When equal dignity occurs, respect for an individual is always present. That's not to say a baby crying for something should always have their wishes met; sometimes it's not appropriate or safe for them to have what they want. The point is that a parent should acknowledge the baby's feelings and help explain to the baby (even if the baby won't fully understand the words yet) why her wishes will not be met, with an empathic response that shows leadership.

Together, with you, your baby learns who they are as an individual. Your baby will learn to be aware of her needs, and how to express them, while also respecting others.

In this Chapter, we will explore the importance of a baby's integrity and finding equal dignity with your baby, which will help your baby grow awareness and self-control, as well as develop a positive self-esteem.

A child is not capable of protecting his integrity on his own, so it's the responsibility of the caregivers to ensure his integrity is respected. Your baby is likely good at expressing his needs and desires, yet he needs an adult's help to ensure that these needs, and wants, do not go completely unnoticed. Of course balancing this will take place, but a baby sharing what they need is important for adults to take note of, and to respond to in a timely way, to show the baby he is heard and cared for.

When done this way, it is a sign to the baby that you are respecting a child's integrity. You're doing this by protecting the baby's personal boundaries and valuing his needs, feelings and desires. Respecting integrity of a baby also means taking a baby's cues seriously, which sends a clear message that the baby, and his inner-self, is valued.

Together with you, your baby will learn about his "inner life" (i.e., how we feel and think) and to navigate needs and wants. Through experience, and by watching his parents' actions, who are his role-models, he learns about respecting integrity.

As it relates to swim class, some examples from the pool could be to respect your baby's wish for a break in communication or activity when they turn their head away. When a baby does this, they are sending a message, "I need a break." Or if your baby is actively looking around, let your baby guide you so that you show him you want to see what he is hoping to explore, up-close, together.

Penelope's Story

Penelope is two-years old. She arrives to her weekly swim class with her Mother, but is not in her usual happy mood today. She clings hard to Mom and is reluctant to go into the water. Her Mother doesn't understand why and thinks maybe she is just "fussing." Her Mom thinks to herself, "we've come all the way here and you love to swim so it'll be ok once you're in the water." In spite of the child's emotional state, Mom puts Penelope into the water, thinking it will be alright.

Suddenly Penelope finds herself not only in the pool, but also in the arms of her teacher. She usually likes to be with her swim teacher, but today she simply doesn't want to be here.

The teacher tries to distract the little girl with a toy, but she just cries. Meanwhile, her Mother sits by the pool, clapping her hands and speaking encouragingly to try and change Penelope's mood, but it doesn't work. Reluctantly, the girl does her best to follow along with the other kids, but she carries on crying. She just isn't happy with the situation she is feeling forced to be in.

Around the pool the children go, under the water and up again, and on every lap Penelope reaches for her Mom. Mom ignores her daughter's cues and keeps clapping, praising Penelope and maintaining a smile, thinking this will bring her comfort and help her adjust.

Things don't get any better. The other children are clearly affected too and the joy from the class is gone. The other children in the class want to help Penelope! The children are in-tune and understand that Penelope needs a change.

The teacher does her best to respect Mom and help keep Penelope calm, but it's uncomfortable.

Penelope's Mother tries her best too (so she thinks), still hoping her daughter will find her good mood. She doesn't want her daughter to miss out on an activity she loves so much.

Needless to say, the rest of the lesson remains uneasy for everyone.

How Would a Grownup Like It?

Picture yourself in Penelope's place. Maybe you are in pain or find yourself with lower energy and it makes you feel depleted. You might choose to stay at home. Or you might choose to go to your swim class, but once there you decide it's too much and you're going to leave. You are in control of your choice.

A child doesn't have the same power to choose and relies on us adults to closely watch their cues, listen to what they are "saying" and do our best to meet their needs.

As a parent, you want to give your child the best possible opportunities in life, and that means tuning-in and adjusting to what your child is able to achieve on a given day.

In the case of Penelope's Mom, she wants her to learn how to swim. It's an important skill and one that she knows will benefit her daughter. Mom also spent a lot of time researching swim prior to signing her up. She found the best swim school, made a financial investment to ensure her daughter is well-rounded, and made a time commitment to be there every week. Part of this time commitment requires Penelope and her Mom to get organized and out the door, on schedule, which can be easier said than done some days!

From Mom's point of view, of course she didn't want Penelope to miss the class over "a little bit of fussing."

From Penelope's perspective, she is a baby focused on how she feels now. She isn't making a mental list and reviewing the many reasons she should be there. She is simply feeling uneasy and knows she wants to be close to her Mom, but not in the water today.

If Penelope's Mom had given her daughter the benefit of doubt, and the comfort of exiting the pool, the little girl would have been happier for it. Ideally, Mom would have taken her daughter out and warmly expressed, "I'm sorry… I thought you'd have fun. What's going on today?" If she didn't respond, Mom could then simply say, "Let's just snuggle here and watch the others… ok?"

Penelope would have felt relieved to know her Mom *heard her, understood her needs and accepted them.* Mom's kind and respectful tone of voice would further instill in Penelope a sense of being seen and loved. By responding to the situation in this way, Mom's message to her daughter is that her inner life and feelings are more important than her performance in the pool. Penelope, upon feeling assured, may have even changed her attitude towards wanting to be in the pool. It's actions like these that ensure a child's integrity is protected and that even at two years of age the child is met with equal dignity.

Note: I travel around the world to teach swimming, with a focus on the relationship of the parent and child. I promote swimming together at all ages, from birth to a comfortable and relaxed swimmer. Penelope's story focuses on a girl that is two-years old. At one of the schools where I was consulting, they had a policy that asked parents to stop swimming with their children at this age. Upon hearing this, and seeing situations like these stories unfold, I explained to the school why I thought it was a mistake and shared the benefits of parents and babies continuing swimming together. They changed their policy upon my recommendation.

Be The Person You Want Your Child to Be

Children learn from their experiences and there is no better way to parent than to model the way you would like your child to be when they grow up. By respecting integrity when a child is little, and unable to do it for themselves, parents are strengthening a child's self-esteem. In doing so, your child will one day be able to protect and respect his own integrity, and the integrity of others.

It's important to keep in mind that babies, children and adults can all have a "bad day." Give your baby room to not feel up to it, and tune-in, the way you would want someone to treat you. A bad day every now and then is not a pattern to be worried about—it's life!

Respect your child's integrity and your relationship will blossom, along with empathy and self-esteem.

Self-Esteem vs. Self-Confidence

Self-esteem and self-confidence are often misunderstood or confused.

Self-esteem is about who you are—the most valuable inherent quality a person can have—and your emotional appraisal of your own worth. It is how a person feels about themself from within. For example, a parent looking to instill self-esteem in their peanut spends time together, shares interest and may say, "I love being here with you. You make me feel so happy. This is a special time for me when we are together." Parents giving their children self-esteem may say, simply, "I love you my dear, because you are you!"

Self-confidence is about what we do. This is also important but it is more centered around abilities, achievements and results. The example from a parent instilling self-confidence is, "Well done! You've learned how to do it!" or "You are the best baby! Look at you swim—you're a pro!"

While both are good, high self-esteem allows someone to be at peace with herself. A person with good self-esteem can more likely conquer various challenges in life because the person is confident from within and has a healthy and realistic view of herself and her abilities. Low self-esteem is often felt like a constant sense of insecurity, self-criticism and guilt. Self-confidence is what a person has when they are good at something, so it can often be restricted to what the person already knows and feels comfortable in.

Words Matter: Speak Thoughtfully to Your Baby

As a parent, or caregiver, it's important to remember to not speak in absolutes—especially negatively towards your baby. For example, "You're always fussing!" or "Why are you cranky all the time?" can impart a negative self-esteem that makes your child question himself. Instead, look to be more concrete and hone in on an issue.

You may instead say, "I can hear you are angry, what's wrong?" or "I can see that there is something bothering you, can I help?" By being open and curious, your child will feel that you are listening and interested in understanding how to help him, and it helps the child to explore his inner life. For your baby, he hears and feels the empathy from you and your honest intentions. This will help him feel secure later in life, too.

As a parent, I also want to caution about finding the right balance for offering praise. While praise is wonderful for parents to give their children, sometimes praise can become harmful to a child's self-esteem and affect a child's willingness to try. Sometimes, when a child receives too much praise, they can become too nervous to fail and stop receiving praise that they give-up before even trying. What can also happen is that because praise is seen as judgemental, a child can become insecure and often seek for outside motivation (whether that is praise, other people's approval, etc.) and validation.

There are many studies that also show that too much reward and praise can actually take away from the experience. The child can become so focused on being praised that they do not find as much pleasure in what it is that they worked for and accomplished.

By sharing interest and giving a more personal response such as, "I know you worked really hard to learn that. I'm very proud of you for trying" or "Did you see how happy you made her when you helped her?" your child will stay connected with a feeling of reward, from within himself, which will also continue an innate desire to stay motivated to learn more.

Your Power

There is a tendency to not always take children's wishes and expressions seriously. Sometimes parents find it frustrating when a child doesn't cooperate with what is expected. I have been there myself and can recount many examples of situations in which parents felt ashamed on behalf of their children, avoided conflict and ended up pushing the kids (and themselves) beyond what is healthy.

Being a parent is demanding at times and always a tremendous responsibility. You are in complete power, all the time (even if it may not always feel that way)!

Ultimately you make all of the decisions, day in and out, for your baby. You shape your child's experience of the world. Because of your relationship, you always are tasked with gauging your little one's reaction and should meet challenges by being flexible and fluid, to ensure you are both happy with the relationship and outcomes of the day.

The more you collaborate with your child, the better your child will be at reaching new levels of self-understanding and self-development.

It takes effort to ensure your child feels seen, heard and understood. You work and learn this together across a range of emotions—from frustration to euphoria. Have you ever had your child begin to fuss or cry and once you react and work with her, her mood changes and all of a sudden she is all smiles, giggles and happy happy?? Yep...success! When you show your child she is valued and loved, she learns to love and value herself. When you love and value yourself, you stand up for yourself when needed and respect others the same way.

79

Integrity and equal dignity leads to tremendous things.

Chapter 9

"I think that everything is possible
as long as you put your mind to it and
you put the work and time into it.
I think your mind really controls everything."
– Michael Phelps

You are Key to Building Your Baby's Resilience

Being resilient means being a strong person. A person that has courage and can stand back up, after they fall, and try again. Building the foundation for resilience starts in the formative baby years and can continue to develop throughout life.

To help cultivate resilience in your baby there are things you can do like creating a nurturing and stable relationship, and being a role-model for how to be resilient. This can be done by you, but also other key people in a baby's life. It's also important to give your baby opportunities to try, practice and learn so they can further develop. All of these experiences and relationships work together to better help a child develop the ability to cope and manage stress. When life brings a child a challenge, they are up to meet it.

Swimming can be a low-stress way to build resilience in the early years. The water is ever-changing and your baby explores his buoyancy as he grows. With your leadership, you and your baby will grow to face challenges together and be stronger for it.

The most important factors in building children's resilience are the stability and commitment of a parent's relationship with their child. This means having a relationship in which you are responsive, protecting your child from harm and providing opportunities for your child to learn within a supportive framework. These attributes all lead to developing a sense of capability and control.

As the leader, you help guide your child while they gradually develop skills such as regulating behavior and adapting to changing circumstances.

Children need to practice anything they are doing. They need to learn to make mistakes and then correct them in order to experience the feeling of success. This can be done with your guidance, but should also be done with some respect to their independence so they learn how to do things for themselves. Of course, what I am suggesting should be appropriate for your baby's age, but the point is that the more a child succeeds on their own, the more self-esteem, confidence and resilience they will build.

As a parent, it is great if you can provide your baby a safe space to experiment and explore. It's not a matter of you taking over. The child must sense that you trust their abilities.

Sometimes all it takes is an encouraging word or sound, a little extra support, or joining in and sharing the child's frustration or pleasure. Eventually you may solve a problem together and then the child will learn to solve the problem on his own, too. It's a step-by-step process. Together.

Using skills we have talked through in earlier chapters, you are already well on your way to having an even stronger relationship with your love bug. This next step is to use your supportive relationship to help your baby build a sense of self-efficacy and perceived control, by providing opportunities to strengthen adaptive skills and self-regulatory capabilities.

Essential Mirroring and Serve and Return

Your child learns by *mirroring* you and also how you communicate and react to one another through the relationship, which is called *serve and return*.

Essential mirroring is when you baby copies what you do. It is a fantastic way for the baby to learn. As a child watches how you respond to a situation, she begins to learn how she should respond to situations herself. The baby learns how to react and how to behave in positive situations and more challenging ones too. The important thing is that watching you teaches your baby that a challenge can have a solution—it just takes a little time to figure out!

Your child also learns when you mirror her. When you mirror her expressions, and put words to the emotion like, "Wow that is hard!" or "Yes, that's the one, you found it!," your child feels your interest and support, and is encouraged to be persistent in a task and to develop trust in her own abilities. How amazing is that?!

Serve and return is another key concept of childhood development and focuses on the relationship give and take. *Harvard University, Center on the Developing Child, explains,*

"Serve and return interactions shape brain architecture. When an infant or young child babbles, gestures, or cries, and an adult responds appropriately with eye contact, words, or a hug, neural connections are built and strengthened in the child's brain that support the development of communication and social skills." It goes on to explain that "much like a lively game of tennis, volleyball, or ping-pong, this back-and-forth is both fun and capacity-building. When caregivers are sensitive and responsive to a young child's signals and needs, they provide an environment rich in serve and return experiences."

Through essential mirroring, and serve and return, resiliency can begin to build in your child. With your caring, confident support, and by leading through examples, you'll inspire your little one to keep trying and to find joy in problem solving. The result will be a resilient child who has peace of mind and the ability to see opportunities beyond any obstacles that may be in their way.

If challenges and problems are something you generally try to avoid, you have a great opportunity to begin to practice tackling them with your child by your side. While building a foundation for resilience is critical at an early age, the process carries on throughout life, affected by both the good and the bad experiences we have. Therefore, it is never too late to cultivate resilience, if that is something you need to work on, and your child will follow your example.

The more you carry yourself as a confident, composed trouble-shooter, the better your child will feel knowing they have the ability to be like you. Your baby will grow in her problem solving cognitive skills, quickly, with your guidance. Your actions will help her little mind grow, knowing she can be just like you. With you as her idol, that is an incredible feeling for your baby to have.

A Lesson from Ella's Story

Thinking back to Chapter 7, and Ella's story about her parents needing to see her side of the "slide experience," there is a great lesson about resilience, too. Through the slide example, there is a balance her parents had to find to respect Ella's wishes, while also doing so with care and support through the process.

Leading by example, her parents showed her that whether she wanted to go down the slide or not, the slide was a safe place—and one that *could* be fun. It was the guidance of her parents that allowed Ella to accomplish something that had initially scared her.

Through that experience she built up confidence and learned that trying things can lead to very positive outcomes.

The process of trial and error helps a child build persistence and perseverance, and the responsiveness from the parents teaches a baby strategies to best take care of their inner-self, which includes being able to know and "voice" saying "yes" or "no" with confidence. In time, as resiliency grows, a child is able to take on larger challenges. This skill-set is invaluable for the rest of a child's life.

Your child wants to be able to do things on their own and he will reach for challenges once he feels ready for them. Exposing your baby to new things is invaluable, but pressuring him into a situation is not. Some children will take longer than others to do something, and every child is different and should go at their own pace. Your role is to continue to provide support and love, and to encourage exploration and learning. It's good to also encourage babies to learn on their own by giving them opportunity and time to explore what piques their curiosity and interest.

Water: An Obvious Playground

As mentioned, being around water and the act of swimming can be a low-stress way to promote resilience in the early years. To build resilience, a child needs to meet challenges outside his own comfort zone and learn by his own experiences to be a problem solver. The water is a great place to do this and as the parent, or caregiver, you can help your baby find the right balance of a challenge. You want to find a challenge that isn't too simple, or too difficult, to allow your baby to accomplish it over time, based on where he is developmentally.

Zone of Proximal Development (ZPD) *is the zone in which your child learns best. This is when your baby has the proper level of challenge, is not yet able to do it, and maybe requires a little support from you. When your baby becomes capable of doing the activity, without support, her comfort zone expands and her self-confidence grows. Your baby will discover she is the kind of person that can learn and do things for herself, building confidence and trust in herself to take on the next challenge! (Ref: Lev Vygotsky)*

The water's ever-changing characteristics provide plenty of opportunities. Most babies learn about their world by putting everything in their mouth, so of course the water in the tub, pool or sea will likely be tasted by your baby. You should anticipate that he might cough, but with time and practice he'll learn how to handle water in and around his mouth.

When he wants to get somewhere, he'll learn that he needs to communicate it to you, and with practice he'll start to move and propel himself through the water to get there.

While he swims it's important that you support him—physically and emotionally. You can help give him the opportunity to do the swimming himself versus overly supporting him, so that he gets the right feedback from the water with his movements.

Your baby may also learn that it's difficult for him to catch a toy in the water, but that through practice he can do it. He may even become a pro at catching toys as they are in motion, bubbling up from the water to the surface.

Isabelle's Story

Isabelle, four months old, is enjoying exploring the water with her Mother.

She is curious about it all. Like most children, Isabelle likes to explore using all her senses—sight, hearing, touch, smell and taste. Balance is also being explored, along with muscle memory and flexibility using the water's buoyancy and pull to challenge the baby and teach her new things.

One day at the pool, Isabelle kept trying to taste the water, getting it in her mouth. Her Mother was getting frustrated with her daughter's repeated attempts and needing to lift her away from it, over and over, for fear of her swallowing the water.

When I see the interaction and ask Mom why she is worried, she replied that she was nervous her baby would get water in her mouth. As a family counselor, my goal with baby swim class is to always help families see the bigger picture. I played "devil's advocate" with Isabelle's Mom to show her how exploration and trial and error are important when the baby is in no real danger.

Our exchange went something like this:

Mom: "I don't want Isabelle dipping her face into the water... she could get water in her mouth."
Me: "Ok, but we know that in small amounts, the pool water is completely safe for babies to digest. So what would be wrong if she drank a little? She's clearly very interested in trying it..."
Mom: "She could swallow the water..."
Me: "...and what would happen then?"
Mom: "She'd start coughing..."
Me: "...and what happens if she coughs?"

By now, Isabelle's Mother has begun to see my point and she relaxes allowing Isabelle to splash and test her boundaries in the water. As Mom expected, it's not long before her prediction comes true: Isabelle takes some water into her mouth and suddenly there's a splutter and a cough. But guess what? Isabelle was okay.

Mom instinctively lifted Isabelle into her arms to help her get the cough out, while also offering her reassurance, restoring her calm and confidence. Soon after, the child was ready to play again and this time as she splashed, Mom and daughter knew there was nothing to be concerned about.

Isabelle eventually got the chance to explore on her own terms and that's how she learned about the appealing aspects of water (and maybe some unappealing ones too—like coughing!). The lesson of being resilient, through trial and error, and the ability to explore was an important experience for her.

There can be situations that trigger fear or insecurity, like a floatation mat, because its unstable surface may make him feel out of balance. With your support and help he will gradually learn to become comfortable and enjoy it.

Swimming Towards Resilience

Isabelle's Mother's concerns are understandable. Plenty of parents worry when their kids are around water, or in any experience that could potentially harm them (which is nearly everywhere!). The fact is, you can't put your children in a bubble, so by being present and offering them safe parameters in all situations, you will be leading the best way possible.

Worrying is not a healthy catalyst for growth and if our children are to become agile "swimmers,"—both in the pool and in life—they will learn how to cope, if we let them. It's our job to give them the chance to learn how to take the responsible measures required in order to be able to *live*.

Learning to swim begins with learning what water is. This is done with the whole body.

It's only natural for small children to learn and explore by putting water in their mouth. Again, they learn through all their senses. Equally important to their learning, is how they watch you behave in the water.

If you, like Isabelle's Mom, seem anxious and you show it by yanking your child out of the pool every time you imagine a "hazard" arising, your child will register that and not learn to deal with water safely and confidently. You could also run the risk of having your child be drawn to danger and test his limits outside of safe boundaries because he feels stifled and wants to rebel.

Smart Parents Raising Smart Children

Studies show that we are programmed by nature to learn from those to whom we are attached. You've likely heard the phrase, "Imitation is the sincerest form of flattery." Well, your children's love and respect for you naturally makes them want to emulate you.

"Leading by example" is also a common phrase. For children, the stronger the connection to their primary person (or people) they have, the more intensely focused they will be to copy what you do. There is a powerful link, a bond, that guarantees a child will learn from their primary person. So it's up to you to show your child how to be the best *they* can be, by being the best that *you* can be.

The Primary People in a Child's Life

Small children learn best from the people closest to them. They generally are closest with one or two people, but a group of key people in a child's life can stretch to also include others who the child spends quality time with.

If you are the primary person, keep in mind that your child is imprinted by everything she sees you do and everything she experiences with you.

Your child is noticing everything about the way you are:

- Your values
- Your willingness and ability to recognize your little one's unique personality
- Your tone of voice and body language
- Your encouragement, or discouragement, of your child's self-exploration
- How you react during less fun situations (for example, taking your child to the doctor for her check-up and shots)
- How you react to your baby when she accomplishes something new
- How you confidently respond when she needs your help

Keep in mind that babies are far more influenced by what we do than by what we say. So when we say one thing, and do another, it is our action that has the clearest message for our little ones.

In addition to watching your actions and communications, your child will also learn through repetition. The combination of repetition, with someone a child feels safe with, is the fastest way for a child to retain information and grow cognitively, emotionally, socially and physically. The more secure a child feels, the more likely he will be to stretch out of his comfort zone and try new things, as he'll be comfortable making mistakes and learning from them to improve, as this child has now grown more resilient.

Chapter 10

"Give the children love, more love
and still more love—and the common sense
will come by itself."
– Astrid Lindgren
(Swedish Author and "Mother"
of Pippi Longstocking)

Creating Emotional Lifejackets

Emotional intelligence is the capacity to be aware of, control and express one's emotions while also being able to handle interpersonal relationships with fairness and empathy.

In today's world there is a great emphasis placed on intellectual intelligence. But rarely do you hear of society actively practicing, or praising children, for their emotional intelligence. This is a skill that is still widely underrated. It's a skill that can significantly help a person throughout life personally (developing self awareness and executive skills) and also socially (with your family, at work, making friends, etc.).

Allan Schore, Developmental Neuroscientist in the Department of Psychiatry at the UCLA David Geffen School of Medicine, said, "In the past, there was an overemphasis in the field of emotion regulation on singularly lowering the baby's distress. But now, we understand that supporting positive emotional states is equally important to creating a 'background state of well-being.' In other words, enjoy your baby. It's protective."

The water allows us to hone in on emotions, and with your baby, you will begin to both become more emotionally intelligent.

Your child is going to experience pleasant and unpleasant feelings, just as you do. That's life. This is not a book about how to avoid exposing your child to unpleasant emotions. It's a book about how to help your child *learn to understand and react to* them. By showing your baby that you can acknowledge a challenging feeling, and not be overwhelmed by it, you can help your baby ease out of feeling badly.

Let's say you're at the pool, and your daughter has spotted a pretty blue ball. She wants to play with it, but it's in another child's hands. You try to give her a different ball, but she angrily throws it away. There's nothing wrong with her desire for the blue ball, and there's nothing wrong with expressing her unhappiness at not being able to have it, but that doesn't change the fact that she simply can't have it right now. It's up to you to acknowledge her feelings, and using your tone of voice also make clear that her desire can't be met right now.

If you can cope with the feeling, you help your child to learn how to cope too. Give her a little time to find her balance again, and she will work through that feeling and be ready to move on.

In other words, a feeling can sometimes be momentarily overwhelming for a child, but you can help them cope. You'll reap the benefits not just in that moment but later on. As children develop the ability to understand and express feelings better, they learn to regulate feelings, too.

Managing pleasant emotions is also important. If your child is joyful, laughing or smiling, join them and experience happiness together!

Emotional Feelings to Be Mindful of During Swim

In baby swimming you can expect, over time, to navigate the entire emotional spectrum. As long as the swim experience is dominated by joy and curiosity, your child will take away positive emotions from learning how to swim, with you by his side.

When I first started my swim school, most parents that came to us for lessons wanted to see their babies "happy." "Happy" for the parents, meant that the babies would swim, with big smiles on their face during every lesson. It's important to understand that children express many emotions and, in fact, a baby who is stimulated and *interested* in an experience is really what parents should be excited to see. Sometimes that includes smiles and giggles, and sometimes the smiles are just on the inside.

Note to parents: An interested expression does not always come off as the expected "happy smile," which can leave some parents worried that their little one is not enjoying the experience. The good news for parents is that when babies are looking around, curious and engaged, they are learning a great deal and soaking in information that help them developmentally. The more parents can understand this, the more they will see the big picture and also see the amazing benefits that are happening while their babies are swimming with them.

Understanding this was also beneficial for the babies, as it gave the babies a chance to see their parents respond, decode and respect a variety of feelings. This was a great learning experience for everyone and we teachers were so proud to be able to focus on the nuances of the relationship, helping parents and babies bond while they became stronger and happier, overall.

Here are some of the main emotions you're likely to encounter while swimming with your baby:

1. Interest: The Key to Knowledge

You know when a child is completely focused. Behaviorally you'll likely notice wide, focused eyes; mouth half open, curious; body pointed towards what they want to learn more about. Often, the pool, ignites this exact response almost immediately within babies.

Sometimes an action will follow (for example, your baby stretches towards the water to touch it), while other times a baby first wants to observe. Both are okay. In fact, many parents have found that a cautious baby at the pool would become extra enthusiastic at bathtime once home, in the baby's well-known environment.

Children are born with a natural drive to explore their surroundings, and to learn and develop their skills. Because of the micro-dynamics of the relationship, it is beneficial when a parent can open up to an experience, as much as their child is, so that it is a shared experience together. Sharing your child's interest helps reinforce it. While swimming with your child (and always) it's best to stay focused and tune out distractions, as this helps your child learn from you and see how to practice these core life skills, which are important for all relationships.

Explore your child's interests, whatever they are, with him. Each child and situation is nuanced and different, so go slowly and stay tuned in to offer emotional support. By being emotionally intelligent, you're allowing your baby to be braver because they have a safety net in you.

2. Joy: A Sure Winner

The body and face are relaxed, the eyes are open, the edges of the mouth are turned upward—your child is glowing with joy. He can't sit still, he simply must move. He feels wonderful all over.

Of the many things that make your child happy, seeing and being with you is one of the most important. When you express happiness, together with your baby, your child's self-esteem will grow. Sharing a positive activity with you enhances his experience of that activity. It is also beneficial to the learning process, creating a positive association in his mind that makes him want to revisit that activity again and again. A happy child is a more effective learner—shared joy strengthens your relationship and gives him a big advantage.

Water offers many ways of having fun together: splashing, jumping, moving in it, tossing a ball and swimming after it. If you consciously emphasize your enjoyment of it and laugh along with your child, he'll come to associate the water environment with joy.

3. Joy from Competence: When a Mission Succeeds

You are supporting your child as she paddles toward a rubber duck that's been difficult to reach. The problem is that as she swims, the motion of the water in front of her pushes the duck farther away. Suddenly she changes tactics—something has dawned on her about the nature of cause and effect. This time she swims toward the toy, but stops for a moment just before reaching it. As the water calms a little, the duck comes within reach, and she manages to get her hands on it.

The feeling of joy, satisfaction and success is clear in her eyes, movement and in her entire body. She glows with pride, her chest held high. She's enjoying the satisfaction of succeeding at something she had struggled with. It's a feeling a child likes to share and have confirmed by adults. An important foundation for self-image, it also helps whet an appetite for further challenges, as the child is resilient.

4. Frustration: An Impetus for Learning

Frustration is a significant driving force in your child's learning and development. You'll see it many times during his childhood and adolescence. A child likes a challenge, but since he's learning, frustration will be part of the process. You may be tempted to help or show him a better way, but too much of that can undermine his self-confidence, leaving him less likely to learn patience and persistence.

The goal is to accommodate any frustration your child may feel, without stepping in to do everything for him. The best way to do this is by encouraging him, by showing interest in how he tries to solve a problem, and by providing step-by-step help if he needs it, while being careful not to simply take over.

This approach supports finding belief in himself and his own abilities, building self-esteem and sets your child up for success the next time he faces a frustrating situation. This also promotes resilience.

5. Fear: Mental Strength

Fear is one of our strongest and most common emotions. It's an important emotion as it serves to protect us, it sharpens our senses and it can trigger a fight, flight or freeze response. Your child will experience fear many times in her life, and, sometimes similar to how an adult may feel at times, fear is not always "real." What I mean is that the feeling is real, but there is no real threat or danger.

It's likely to happen when she experiences loud noises, feels a sudden movement or finds herself in unfamiliar, unpleasant surroundings/situations, or with unfamiliar people. If something becomes unpleasant or is a real threat, move your child away from the danger. When there is no real threat, with your empathetic support, guidance and your child's own practice, your baby will expand her comfort zone and learn how to handle a fearful situation by developing greater mental strength.

A scared child stares and gets stiff and tense in the body, as her heart rate increases. If the source of the fear doesn't go away, she will often begin to cry. In a situation she finds hard to interpret, she'll move close to you or seek out your eyes. If you nod in reassurance, and smile to show there's no threat, she'll know she can relax. It's crucial to remember that your child can also get scared if *you* get scared.

The whole experience of learning to swim may create challenging situations for a child, which makes it an ideal context for her to feel your predictable and dependable support, and gradually learn how to confront fear.

To a child, each swim class can have elements and situations that are frightful for her. Any number of things from jumping into the water, a new swim teacher, an illness or having a routine changed can shake up your baby's world. A little baby may express some apprehension and a bigger need for closeness and support if something like this were to happen, so it is important to go at manageable pace for your child.

Part of the challenge is figuring out just what level of excitement your child can tolerate. There is a balance between excitement and fear. When she is afraid, try to find the cause and acknowledge it, as no one learns very well when they are scared. If the cause of the fear is not actually dangerous, your support and loving arms will show her there's nothing to fear and help her ease out of being worried.

Teaching Children to Believe in Their Own Abilities: When a situation becomes too much for your child, he will turn away from it or come closer to you. The signals of discomfort will be there, some of them silent, and you need to try and decode them so you can respond appropriately. Slow down the pace of activity and get closer. When your response is the right one, you'll feel your child calm down and soon he'll want to get back into the action.

Your child will always be testing and developing his mental muscles. If he knows you will be there when he needs help, he will have faith in his ability to tackle challenges. A lack of parental support, on the other hand, or too much pressure to take on fears and challenges, can undermine self-esteem and confidence. It can leave a child frightened and insecure, stunt his emotional development and interfere with his ability to learn.

6. Crying: Help Me!

Sometimes it's hard to know why a small child is crying. The problem may be physical: hunger, overstimulation, fatigue, cold, pain; but it may also be emotional: anger, fear, confusion. Whatever the reason, the one thing you know for sure is that she's telling you she's experiencing something she cannot resolve on her own. Your baby needs you. Sooth your baby when she is crying and help her make sense of what is happening by being the helpful guide, by her side.

Occasionally you simply must try and guess what the cause of the tears are and how to remedy it. A child who cries in the pool may be overwhelmed by input from all the senses, as well as new sensations, which may be confusing to process. Keep your baby close to you, and turn away from the source of stimulation, which will help make her world smaller and more manageable. Once you notice that she has relaxed again, you can try to initiate some kind of activity, she may even seek out to do this for herself.

Are You Afraid of Water?

Humans are cleverly designed to trust those who care for us. We adopt their instincts and do as they do; evolution dictates that this is a good survival strategy. When your child is small and inexperienced, he's more susceptible to the influence of your feelings and reactions. Therefore, remember that you need to be aware of your own feelings: If you are irrationally insecure around water, take responsibility for it and do your best to not pass that worry on to your child. He was not born afraid of water; on the contrary, before his birth, he lived for months in water, in the womb, and he most likely still feels at home with the warmth of water surrounding him.

My advice if you do have fears about the water is to discuss it with the swim school teacher. My hope is that the teacher can help you relax by providing you good support so that you can also experience a feeling of the water being a safe and wonderful place. It will make it easier for you to be attentive to your child's emotions, even when you may feel a little uncertain yourself.

We instinctively avoid danger and as parents we aim to protect our little ones from anything that might hurt them or make them afraid. Fear can have many sources and not everything that scares us is actually dangerous; sometimes it's merely unfamiliar. It's important that we learn to look fear in the eye and teach our kids to tell the difference between what's actually dangerous and what may only be the unknown, which is *interesting and new*.

Some children are more fear-prone than others and need a little more support and encouragement in tackling what frightens them. Without it, they may find themselves held back by those fears later on.

The Inner Compass

Emotions have no gender, age or race. They are neither right nor wrong. They are just *there*, in all of us. Emotions always carry a message, as they're trying to tell us something. To become self-aware and to control our emotions is a core life skill. The more emotionally intelligent we become, the better our emotions will serve us in life. Children express their emotions with no filter, and they need a caring adult to help them sort their emotional "inner compass." Unfortunately, some people can still give the impression that some emotions are acceptable and others are not. That idea can have a negative impact. A child who is told "there's nothing to be sad about" or "calm down," doesn't learn to understand the emotions of grief and anger. Additionally, statements like these made by a caregiver lack empathy for the child and do not respect the child's integrity. The more a parent or caregiver acts in this manner, the more likely a child will learn to suppress emotions. This can result in uncontrollable explosions of emotion from time to time.

The idea of unacceptable emotions can also cause problems in the long term. A child whose emotional needs seem to be ignored, over and over, will not learn to trust himself, and his inner compass may drift off the mark. Mistrusting one's emotions can even extend to mistrusting the body, failing to face basic issues of physical or emotional pain head-on.

I urge you to pay attention to both your emotions and those of your baby. The more in-tune you are, the stronger your relationship will be. The more emotionally intelligent you become, the better you will be to face any situation, head on, with your baby who is becoming more emotionally intelligent, too, with your guiding.

Chapter 11

"Happiness is when what you think, what you say,
and what you do are in harmony."
– Mahatma Gandhi

HAPPY

It's almost time to take the plunge into Part 2 of the book, which gives you activities to do in the water, with your baby.

Before we get started, I wanted to recap much of what we discussed in the book, to help keep you and your baby on track for happiness, through the gift of swim.

These cues are meant to be a mindset for you to focus on ahead of getting into the pool, or open waters (if you are lucky enough to be traveling, or live in an environment that has warm enough waters to swim with your baby).

Follow these five simple steps and you and your child will soon be enjoying the gift of swim and working towards a stronger relationship!

Ultimately, swim will lead you and your baby towards the most important feeling of all—the feeling of being understood. To understand, and to be understood, leads to another feeling. The feeling of being HAPPY.

Help guide your child in the water, and remember the importance of self-exploration!

Activities, like swim, need routine and repetition for a young baby's mind to grow.

Present parents and caregivers, who are tuned-in, develop deep bonds and trust with their babies.

Playing is key! Take time to make games out of activities in the water and have fun together.

You are the leader! Your baby is watching you, so be emotionally intelligent to guide your baby, while also ensuring a safe and positive environment for the two of you, as you learn together.

Now it's time to swim with your baby. Let's dive in...

Part 2 of the book is filled with activities that are meant to provide you with lots of fun and enjoyment. These are based on my many years of experience with baby swimming— it's my way of taking you to my swim school in Sweden. Whether you find a swim school that practices this relationship-focused approach to swim or you follow these teachings directly in your own pool, implementing the concepts in this book will empower you to get the most out of your swim experience.

I wish you and your little one many good experiences in the water, as you enjoy swimming together.

PART 2

Let's Swim!

In the first portion of this book, we examined childhood swimming from an emotional and social perspective, with the emphasis around the relationship between you and your baby. My baby swimming ideology supports building upon core developmental needs that help you and your baby have a relationship that will flourish, using the wonderful activity of swim to learn more about yourself and your baby and bring you closer together. The core fundamental points outlined in Part 1 are key to understand in order for you to be as prepared as possible, mentally, before getting into the water. As you practice what is outlined, my hope is that you will notice positive changes in and between you and your baby, in the water and on land.

The stronger your emotional, mental and social foundation is, the stronger and healthier your relationship will be to create a new kind of happy, for everyone involved. This happiness is within the individual, as well as through various relationship dynamics.

Now that you have a deeper knowledge and have completed the "mental training," to help your baby in the water, it's time to learn the "physical training" and swim!

Throughout Part 2, I will teach you all kinds of swimming activities with the recommended age to start indicated for each activity. While the motions of swimming in the water are a key part of Part 2, I will also always remind you how to maintain the focus on the connection, togetherness and growth you and your baby need to have while swimming.

Also in this section, I've outlined swim stages by average age developmental levels, to help guide you, but remember to tune-in and be mindful of YOUR baby's needs and where *they* are developmentally. No baby is "behind," rather they may just need more time to grow and learn before they are ready for the next level of swim stages outlined on the following pages. Go at your baby's pace, without judgement or fear of being behind. Eventually all babies end up swimming if we give them the possibility to practice. Take solace in knowing you and your baby are exactly where you're supposed to be.

When combined with the knowledge from Part 1, Part 2 is both functional and fun. It has many examples of ways you can physically support your baby through activities and swim holds that I have done in my classes for more than 25 years. These activities can be used as a guide for your swimming journey with your baby, from birth to two-years old.

I hope you are ready for bubbles, splish-splashing, floating, giggles and smiles. Let's swim to greater happiness!

Introduction to
Swimming by Developmental Levels

Babies progress at rapid rates cognitively, physically and emotionally. While every baby indeed grows at a very fast pace when you are considering the changes occurring, every baby reaches developmental milestones in their own time. Some faster, some slower, and some on target with a pediatrician's average growth charts, which measure height and weight, as well as different motor and cognitive milestones by the medium age.

A Note to Parents:

Children who are born prematurely, or who have mental or physical limitations, often benefit greatly from baby swimming, but there may be special considerations to make. If your child was born prematurely and/or if your child has a chronic illness or other kind of limitation, always consult with your child's doctor before you begin swimming.

For premature babies, if you're lucky enough to have a high quality swim school, with facilities that accommodate the needs of a more sensitive baby who was born early, then when your little premie is healthy, thriving and weighing more than 4 kilograms (9 pounds), swimming should pose no problem. However, children born prematurely and coming into the world only weighing 1.5kg (3.3 pounds), and under, will still be immature in areas and may need extra caution or considerations, even once they meet the weight suggested. In this case, I recommend you always consult your child's pediatrician before starting to swim.

From Splashes to Baby-Freestyle:
Mapping Your Babies Aquatic Progress

I've broken down five levels to consider while you are swimming with your baby. You'll see that I have age guidelines next to each level, but again, go at your baby's pace.

Level 1: Tuning-In: At Home in the Bathtub
Level 2: Learning as a Team: First Experiences in the Pool
Level 3: Exploring Abilities and Possibilities
Level 4: Together Towards Independence
Level 5: Bigger Adventures

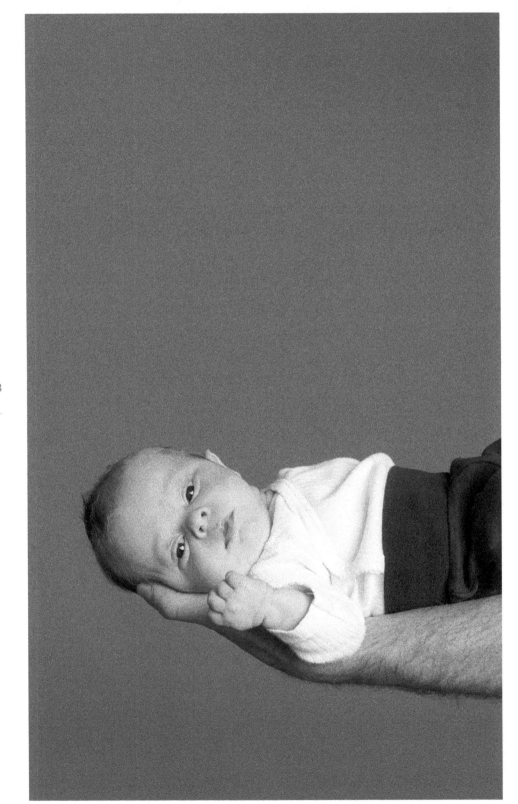

Level 1: Tuning-In: At Home in the Bathtub
0–2 months

For your baby, the world is new and there are so many different sensations to take in. Lucky for your little bundle of love, he has you. Your baby learns through experiences, and the direct contact with you and other loved ones, ensuring he has plenty of enjoyable contact and stimulation throughout the day.

As it relates to your baby experiencing the sensation of water with you, the best way to introduce your baby to H_2O is by giving him a soothing, warm bath.

Baths at home can be enjoyed right from birth. You may decide to take a bath with your baby, in a full-size tub, or use a baby tub that fits in a sink or in the bathtub. The idea is to give your baby the experience of being in the water, with you there to comfort him to ensure he feels safe.

You can choose to give your baby a bath at any time of day. Personally, I enjoyed giving my children an evening bath as it is an excellent way to enjoy each other's company, play together, relax and become "pleasantly tired" before bedtime.

Creating an evening ritual often contributes positively to family life overall. Not only can a warm bath make your child tired, it can also satisfy his need for activity, proximity, togetherness and loving care. All of these feelings help prepare children for a good night's sleep, as they settle down for the night.

When you think about your newborn, remember that for the last nine months (give or take), your baby lived in water! With this in mind, in your safe hands, a "liquid environment" is extremely appealing to most infants. It may take one or two bath experiences for you and your baby to adjust, but once you hold your baby relaxed and comfortably in the water, he will likely grow to enjoy bath time with you.

If you can, I recommend you try to get into a bathtub with your baby, to bathe together. He will enjoy the feeling of being enveloped in even more warm water, well supported by your arms and hands, while he either floats on his tummy, side or back.

For many babies, the position of laying on their back while looking up at your face, is a favorite position. As you do this, you may be rewarded with your baby's first smile! Your face is important to your baby and the combination of the emotional response you give, with the sensory experience he will get in the water, promotes organizing emotional development in a joyful way.

Calm, rhythmical motion through the water is also comforting for newborns. Try swaying your baby gently, while he is resting on his back, as you support him under his head. If you have a big bathtub, you can also swing your baby gently from side to side, or slowly rock from back to front, safely supporting him while he feels the shifts and the water caressing his body.

Tune-in to your child's experience and how he responds to the bath. Like a dance, you'll lead and then it's good to also let your baby lead, as you share in the experience together. Find the rhythm that feels good to you both and pay close attention to your baby's needs so that you are active or resting, when needed. Over time, you will become more aware of small signs and quick shifts in your baby's mood and will be able to meet those needs faster. Your baby will feel safe, relaxed and ready to explore the water with you as the confident parent guiding him. That strong bond and trust is invaluable and a bath is a perfect place to start the beautiful journey of being in the water, together.

Pro tips:

- It's important to understand that newborns regulate contact and stimuli by turning their head away when they've reached their limit, so watch for that behavior and give them a break, when they need it. This is a good exercise to become aware of in helping to create boundaries and being mindful to respect your baby. Soon enough, they'll be ready to play again. Go at their speed and you'll be rewarded for the effort.

- Once your baby weighs 4 kilograms (9 pounds) and his belly button has healed, he is ready to begin baby swimming (if you feel comfortable and ready), as long as the conditions are suited for a sensitive infant (see page 132-133).

  - For Mothers it might take a few extra weeks (6-8 weeks) before joining in a pool with your baby, maybe sooner, pending your doctor's recommendation.

- When you are washing your child's hair or face, communicate so she always is prepared and can get ready for what is about to happen. This is respectful, provides predictability and also offers a sense of control for your baby—all things that meet basic human needs. By tuning-in to your baby you can make taking a bath about teamwork, tear-free.

Do not submerge your child in the bathtub. Instead let your child take the initiative to do so, when they are ready. In the context of a positive and predictable relationship, there will come a day when your child's desire to explore will lead her to submerge in the bathtub in the absence of any external pressure and this is the best way.

Level 2: Learning as a Team: First Experiences in the Pool

3–6 months

Your baby's neck and back are growing stronger during these months and she'll be better equipped to hold her head up, with less support from you. This means you'll probably make adjustments in the way you support her while in the water. It also is a good time to introduce your baby to a pool that meets the standards and needs for baby swimming.

Additionally, once you're at this stage, "tummy time" becomes an important position on land. Some babies do well with it and others aren't keen on it, but it really is vital in helping to grow your baby's motor skills. Tummy time is key because it helps strengthen neck muscles, arm muscles and is the gateway for crawling. In the water, tummy time has greater odds of being a pleasant experience for your baby due to her ability to float and feel weightless. Plus, when you are in a pool with your baby, you're at eye-level, which imparts a feeling of connection during the activities like tummy time.

Once in the pool, depending on you baby's personality, you will see how she either observes everything that is going on around her, remaining reserved, or if she chooses to engage more actively with the water and make direct contact.

You will also notice when your baby needs a break, because she will come close to you and relax before wanting to explore again. By being in the water, it offers a great way of learning your baby's rhythm. As you swim together, remember that while all these sensations are familiar to you, your baby is exerting a lot of energy to absorb lots of new information. Take the time to enjoy the experience and give your baby what she needs, as you swim together.

Introduce Toys, With You Being
the Most Important Part of Swimming

At three to six months, your baby starts to move her arms and legs with more precision. Because of this, toys can be fun to introduce in small volumes. The most important "toy" is you. Being connected and focused on the relationship is always ideal, but some toys can be a fun addition that promote positive outcomes for the baby and your relationship.

In the water, toys stimulate vision, coordination and depth perception. They also present challenges since it's not easy to grasp a toy moving in water. That extra challenge often makes it even more interesting for your baby. Toys also promote teamwork and you can help your child build core life skills such as focus. Together, you will practice working as a team to accomplish a task (e.g., "hunting" for a moving toy and finally getting it!) and experience joy in succeeding together.

At around five months, your baby will start finding her feet very interesting. *Fun fact: a baby often will hold their feet, while on their back, completely engaged by the experience. For any Yogi's out there, this position is called, "Happy Baby" pose, and there are additional poses you can do in the water to mirror this!*

Learning to sit is another advancement that often occurs during this age. By using poses in the water that mirror what your baby is learning to do on land, she will feel she has a choice in the flow of swim, which will deepen trust and promote greater learning.

Level 3: Exploring Abilities and Possibilities
7–9 months

A babies' desire and need to explore the world is strong at this age, as they are eager to test their own abilities.

During this phase, as it relates to swimming, your baby can usually stay engaged in an entire swim class session (which generally lasts about 30-45 minutes). If you are teaching your little one in a home pool, you can strive for this same length of time, but know that if your baby seems tired earlier then that is completely normal. It's completely okay to take a break or be finished with swim for the day if your baby is done. Listening to your baby's energy level and meeting his needs is always most important for swimming, or any activity.

Similar to Level 2, you will notice even more motor advancements in Level 3 making their way from land, into the water. For example, if your baby is starting to crawl or walk, you'll see motions similar in the water while he is "swimming freestyle" (with your support, of course).

Always cooperate with your baby's movement so your little swimmer gets true feedback from the water and a feel for the effect of his movements. Adding songs, activities and guidance along the way will help him develop his skills even more. Saying that, a body righting reaction will emerge sooner or later that counteracts the flow and fluency, in his free swimming. When this happens, flow with your baby and guide him with energetic empathy back into the more effective horizontal swimming position. Ultimately, you want your baby comfortable and feeling good in the water. When you cooperate well together, your baby will explore and learn about the feeling of resistance, balance and his buoyancy in the water. Through trial and error your baby will learn about physics and how the water can work to his advantage.

Using you as support to help your baby is important, but you never want to force your peanut into a static position for too long. If your child's instinct is to be on his tummy— or back—let him be there. You can try guiding him into flipping back and forth gently, while keeping eye contact and a positive, helpful expression that shows him you're in it together. Your teamwork has only grown stronger, after all, in these months, so he knows he can depend on you to guide him.

My last recommendation for swimming during this developmental level is to spend as much time in a horizontal position as possible, as this is the best position for your baby to develop his swimming.

Level 4:
Together Towards Independence
10–12 months

Children who have been swimming for some time usually can anticipate their next trip to the pool or swim class. For a child that loves the time together with you in the water, you'll notice she can't wait to get into the pool. She'll show this by doing things to help get ready such as finding her bathing suit or gathering toys. Let your child help, to give her a positive feeling of self-reliance and responsibility. Danish Family Therapist, Jesper Juul, once said, "overly helpful parents, tend to raise helpless children." Help your child be strong by welcoming the initiative when she attempts to try new things, so that she can practice and learn. By parenting in this way, you add meaning to an effort and also allow for more fun to take place by showing your baby that trial and error is a part of life. A child this age can also get frustrated if they're not given the chance to do things independently. Flotation aids like balancing rings and pool noodles, if used in moderation, can increase your baby's freedom, allowing her to swim, turn around and move independently in the water with you as a companion.

If your child is standing at this age, having an area that is shallow enough that she can touch the floor is fantastic! It will allow her to walk or crawl around and feel how water has an effect on her movements, without your support. It is also a good place for exploring the idea of "breaking the surface." An example of this might be bending down into the water to retrieve something she can see (e.g., a diving toy) or swimming from the shallow end to you (even if it is a very short distance). Not all swimming pools offer a shallow area, so an alternative place can be a staircase area where your child can explore the different depths at the steps.

Together, as you and your baby explore, engage in activities with your little one by talking to her and mimicking her actions in the water. If she splashes, smile and splash too! If she moves, move with her, while you share her excitement. Make it a safe, fun place for her. She will love seeing that you are as enthusiastic about the experience as she is.

At this level, song activities together are also excellent and offer great development opportunities on many levels—socially, cognitively, emotionally and intellectually. It's good to select songs that are related to the movements you are doing in the pool, so you can coordinate movements and your baby starts to recognize what to do during points in the song.

Balancing activities are also great fun and promote physical development and strength (see page 162).

Water is so full of possibilities to a child that even just pouring it out of one object and into another can be an absorbing activity. Cups, buckets and jugs—as simple as they are—can be a great source of fun, not to mention an excellent way to be introduced to the laws of physics. For this age group, and older, in my classes I create "The Science Station" where children explore through various activities, like using a water-vessel to play in different ways. Sometimes a baby enjoys this experience as much as being in the pool itself.

From finding toys under the water's surface, to swimming a short distance, to other fun, your baby will love growing with you in the water! Practice makes perfect and because a baby's memory doesn't last very long at this age, remember to make swimming a routine and be consistent with the frequency. You can also create delightful routines and rituals in the water so your baby has the best chance of learning and absorbing the skills she's learning each week.

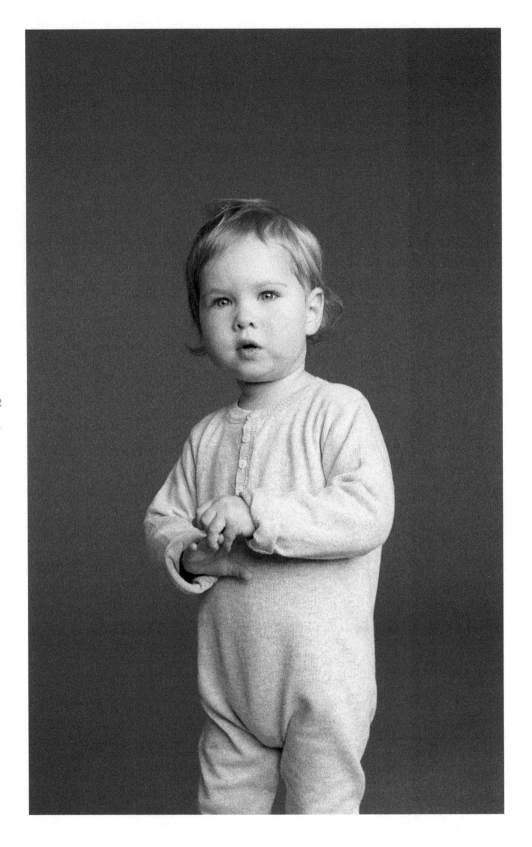

Level 5:
Bigger Adventures
1–2 years old

New developments in motor skills that happen during the second year of life give your baby new opportunities to move more, and farther, independently. Water offers fantastic opportunities for strengthening, stimulating and challenging your baby during this stage.

The world is rapidly becoming bigger for your baby. Don't be surprised to find when you are swimming that your child suddenly develops an interest in the world outside the pool, too. From your perspective that may be a little frustrating—especially if you have joined a pool/swim school. You don't want to go through the effort of getting your baby into the water just to have them want to be outside of it! Remember that curiosity will reign supreme and it's best to respect your child's interest and be flexible. Look to find balance in letting your explorer roam, but also engaging him in the water, with you by his side the whole time.

Guide him in new swim activities that are more advanced. Be mindful that while your baby has grown exponentially, he is still little and may not be able to do many of the activities without your support and watchful eye, keeping him safe. Help your baby to be adventurous try new things, but do not push or withhold your baby to do more than he is ready to handle.

The shallow area of a pool continues to be useful to your child at this stage, providing exciting experiences as it relates to exploring buoyancy and finding balance.

Watch how your child explores and becomes more aware of his body and how it works in water. He will begin to understand what happens in the water, while he is moving, and how those movements and balance differ from what he does on solid ground.

At some point you may find your child trying to push your hands away as you are supporting him in the water. Your instincts will probably tell you that even though that's what he wants, you shouldn't let go. My advice in this scenario is to find a happy medium that is safe, but that also respects your child's desire to do more on his own. For example, if he is comfortable submerging you may give him the opportunity for a short swim where he wants to swim or to the steps area and then give him freedom to explore where he can stand, without you supporting him. This is the road from fully dependent, to gradually growing into healthy independance.

You can expect that your child will experience growth spurts and plateaus in his development. I often joke with parents that even if their baby took to water very well and was an "advanced" swimmer in early months, that it is too soon to get excited that they have the next Olympian on their hands. Always remember that being in the water is so much more than just swimming. Take time to experience and enjoy the gift of swim and don't worry about how "good" your child is. They will have spells of rapid growth, and regression, so ride the wave with them and be patient. Be fluid, the way water is, and encourage positivity.

As your child gets close to two-years old, he will be very mobile—and much stronger— making him more capable of new activities! At this age, your child will be getting better at combining actions in sequences and will likely enjoy his growing capabilities to the fullest.

Your step-by-step support is the best way to make him feel your cooperation, trust and encouragement and make it possible for him to gradually take over and do the many swim activities on his own, with his trusted guardian by his side.

Swim Into Happy

We ended Part 1 of the book with an acronym, H.A.P.P.Y., to help remind you of the steps towards the best mindset you can have before you and your baby get into the water.

Now that we're in Part 2 of the book, I've created another acronym to remind you of your approach once you're in the water. S.W.I.M.

After all, HAPPY babies SWIM.

See each other at eye-level.
This creates a deeper connection and allows your baby to mirror experiences and receive emotional feedback, as you discover swimming together. Don't be surprised if your baby is busy looking at everything but you—there is, after all, a lot to take in. Following her gaze will clue you in about what interests her. See how your baby interacts and explores the world and you will learn to know your baby on a deeper level, all of which will strengthen the bond between you.

Always position yourself so that your eyes can easily meet. When your child is on her tummy, drop down to that level, with your shoulders at the surface of the water. When she's on her back, stand up so that your baby can easily look around and easily find you. In general, give her your undivided attention in the water and use eye-contact to help show that you're present.

Water is your friend.
Don't be hesitant or fearful of the water. See the many advantages and positive advancements that can take place for your relationship with your baby, as well as other developmental areas. Use the knowledge you now have from this book to show your baby the water is something you can both enjoy together.

Take the time to familiarize both of you with the role of natural buoyancy in all your water activities, whether they involve motion or are just supportive holds.

Give your child plenty of time on his back or tummy, as it builds water intelligence and leads towards swimming on his own.

Let your baby feel how the water buoys him up and feel how little support from you is required in the water.

As you enter the water, you support your baby in a different way than you would on land. You want your little one to be in a swimming position and to let the feeling of buoyancy be the experience, as you both become more comfortable moving through the water.

Interact through play!

When all is said and done, there's little point in swimming with your baby if you are not going to have fun. I recommend you make play an indispensable part of your time in the water, whether it springs from your child's own spontaneous activity or from activities orchestrated by you or the teacher.

Remember that we play for play's sake and we all play in different ways throughout our life. Your child learns about herself, others and the world around her through play. Play also reduces stress, as does laughing—so enjoy the water! (*See page 128-129 for more information on how flotation devices, games, toys and singing can be incorporated.*)

Move with the water and in-tune with your baby

To move is to learn. Your child needs plenty of opportunities to move in various ways and directions in the water. You enable that for him. Be aware of how you support your baby and make sure to give your child the opportunity to move his entire body as freely as possible.

This means that the various ways you support him should not be too restrictive. When your little one sees something and starts to move, support him by following along. Flurries of activity will alternate with short periods of calm during which your baby is resting and reflecting in the safety of your arms. When he's ready to move again, move with him!

Swinging and swaying in the water generates a soft, massaging sensation over your child's body, which in turn will either relax him or stimulate his desire to initiate his own movements in the water.

As you move in-tune with each other, you'll experience an unspoken understanding and become in sync through rhythm. This "waltz" is contagious and will strengthen your relationship.

When introducing new activities and positions, always keep your movements slow and tune-in to your child's pace. If you go too fast, it may disrupt your baby's balance or make it difficult for him to learn. Slower, more deliberate motions lets your baby follow what is happening and maintain his equilibrium. A child that is balanced is a much better learner. As your child learns the movements you can pick up the pace together.

- **Games**

  You and your baby can make a game out of nearly any activity in the water. Playing together will heighten the joyful, emotional experience you will have, strengthening your bond and leading to a healthy, happy relationship.

  Games can be anything: examples include blowing bubbles, bobbing, splashing and moving fast through the water (with a cheerful *swoosh!*), followed by moving slowly (while whispering "swoosh!") to allow your baby to feel the difference in movement and sound. Give your baby time to see if she imitates these motions and begins to interact with the water directly.

  Just as you talk to your baby on land, it's great to attach words to actions in the water. For example, "Look at Daddy's splashing!," "Mama's making bubbles!," or "Olivia is swimming!". All these activities, and associated words, help her learn about her world, support language development and distinguish herself from other people so she begins to get a sense of who she is.

  Later, the peek-a-boo activity becomes a fun game as you can hide under the surface of the water, returning with a smile to your child's relieved, happy face!

  Exploring colors and shapes can also be fun. Be creative and have fun with the games—you'll be laughing and smiling together in no time at all!

- **Toys**

  Almost any kind of object can be turned into a toy: jugs, buckets, cups, mugs, balls, balance rings, pool noodles, foam floating mats, etc. Whatever object a child can grab, throw, push, pour water from or into and out of, stack up, float or sink can become a "toy." Your child will grab it, taste it, suck on it and bite it, later throw it, sit on it, kick it and every other treatment you can think of. As he plays with the object, the "toy" will be teaching him about various properties and uses.

  Pay attention to how he tests the toys and watch as the toy stimulates his senses. You may even want to deliberately awaken his interest in a particular object by playing with it yourself. Often when a child sees someone else with a toy, it makes them more interested in that particular toy. This can be a good time to start teaching what sharing is, and as always, it starts with you role-modelling how to give.

- **Singing**

  Has music ever moved you? Not in the physical sense, but emotionally? Music has a magical effect on us, as it can support our rhythm of movement, while also being soothing or energizing depending on the beat.

  Songs, and the act of singing, can elevate something ordinary into joyful play. With this in mind, adding music to the pool is a great idea!

  My years of experience found that singing different songs, at the same time for different swimming activities, helps babies retain information and learn to anticipate what's coming up next in a swim class routine. It offers important predictability and the possibility of deeper learning for a child. I recommend you create songs for the start of swim, songs for different activities and then also a song to help prepare your child to end swim time. Tailor the songs to the activity and your child so it's possible for her to join in, if she is old enough. Some songs will be happy and familiar such as a "welcome to swim" song with your child's name. Others may be energizing and catchy, and some can be more calming, like when a baby is floating and it's time to relax.

  Music and dance creates bonds because synchronized movement is a language of its own. It helps guide behavior and create connection without saying anything, and when you move in sync with someone it gives the feeling of being part of something bigger.
  Singing also supports and promotes language development, through the rhythm, as well as the relational and emotional aspects of a relationship.

  Your child will love hearing you sing, so put your heart into it—don't worry about being off-key! Have fun and enjoy singing together.

- **Flotation Devices**

  A flotation device, such as a Pool Noodle or Swim Ring, can give a child freedom to move around independently in the water. But too much time spent with flotation devices can adversely impact muscle memory and your child's swimming, so use these aids in moderation.

  A great reason to use one is so you and your baby can independently swim side by side, playing with freedom, speed and direction.

Swimming Essentials:
Safety Needs and Tips for Swim

Before getting into the water there are a few things to be mindful of to ensure it's a safe environment and that you, and your baby, are prepared. Baby swimming does require some extra prep work, so below is a checklist of items to help make it simple for you.

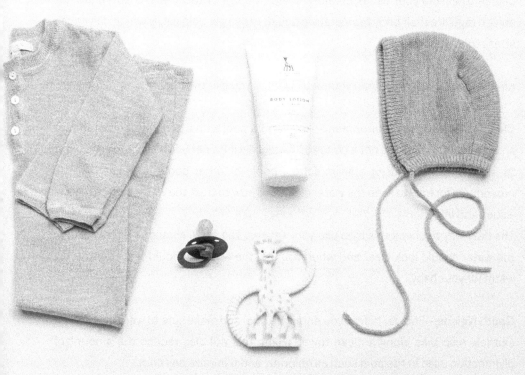

A well-packed swim bag

- Swimwear for you and your baby. There is special swimwear for babies and you should choose one that has lining and that is close fitting to your baby's thighs and tummy. Some swim schools require a swim diaper under the swim pants for extra precaution.
- Clothes for your child that are easy to take off and put on again.
- Your child's pacifier, if used.
- Towels for both baby and you.
- Swimming goggles for the adult, if you like.
- Oil or lotion for the child's skin *after* the swim lesson.
- Food and drink for your child to have before / after swimming.
- Something to drink for yourself. It is especially important if you are breastfeeding to stay hydrated.
- Extra diapers—regular for after class, and special diapers for the pool.

Pool Basics

- **Keep it warm** -Your child needs a pool temperature of 32°–35°C (90°–95°F) and a warm, draft free environment. This temperature may seem high, but it's the right degree to ensure your baby's comfort. Under the age of two-years, children are not able to regulate their body temperature and they can get cold easily which can cause stress to their bodies.

  Keep a towel close by to wrap your baby in once you exit the pool.

- **Clean water and pool environment**—You want a pool with a good hygienic standard so that health issues are not a concern. Especially if it's not your own pool, you want to make sure the staff of a swim school pool—or other pool—is diligent on the procedures for how to keep the water clean and how to treat the water to avoid safety issues and infections.
  The best way to check this is to use your senses. The smell shouldn't be too strong, the water should look clear and when you feel the water it should feel comfortably warm for your baby.

- **Good Hygiene**—Shower before you enter the pool and make sure to wear clean swim clothes. Also take along a clean towel. Doing this will also reduce the amount of disinfection used in the pool such as chlorine, and minimize any odor.

- **Keep it calm**—A young child is sensitive to sensory input. Too much noise and different activities, can make it hard for a young baby to focus. Calm environments are the best places to learn and absorb information.

- **Limit time**—To avoid chilling (even in warm pools) and overstimulation, which can affect your child's ability to concentrate and learn, swimming times should be limited. I recommend 30 minutes of swim (or less) for babies that are newborn to six-months old and up to 45 minutes of swim (or less) for babies that are six-months and older.

- **Always stay close to your child**—This probably goes without saying, but you should never leave your child alone by the pool. And even if you are present, you should not take your eyes off of them. Children are naturally curious and want to explore, but it is your role to keep them safe by guiding them towards fun activities and away from any danger. An adult should always be with a child in the water, or at arm's reach depending how old and comfortable of a swimmer the child is.

- **Keep it healthy**—A child who is feverish, or generally not in good health, should avoid the pool. Swimming, and the stimulation that accompanies it, uses energy, and when your child is sick his energy should be channeled toward getting well. Furthermore, you don't want to risk exposing others to infection.

Note: especially in colder climates, a runny nose is common and does not necessarily mean your child has an infection. As the parent or guardian you need to use your judgement to determine if your child is healthy enough to swim and doesn't have an infection.

Respiratory Conditions: Swimming for children and adults with asthma can have wonderful benefits as the water pressure and activity of swimming can strengthen the respiratory system. It's important to be aware of your baby's proneness to asthma and to be mindful of certain medications he may be taking to help the condition. Some medications can affect the "protective respiratory reflex," so introducing a baby to submerging under water is not advisable if your child is on such medication. However, a child who can already submerge (before being introduced to this medicine, if asthma happened later in life) should not be affected and can swim above and under the water's surface, as normal.

Skin: A child with sensitive skin, or skin conditions such as allergies or eczema, can most often swim. Swimming itself does not cause sensitive skin or eczema, but the water has a drying effect that can make the skin extra-sensitive. In most cases, a good quality lotion or oil can remedy this when applied after swimming. Please don't apply lotion just before going into the pool, as doing so can make your baby slippery, and the chlorine can react in a way that may result in itchiness or a rash.

Chlorine can agitate pale, delicate or other types of sensitive skin, causing redness and itching, even in low concentrations of chlorine. Any redness should abate without after-effects in a matter of hours.

Safe entry

Built-in stairs: If there are stairs leading down into the pool, use them. As you enter the water, hold your baby close to you with her tummy against your chest so she feels secure. Make sure you are able to support her head against your shoulder. If your child is a little older, she will probably enjoy watching the action from the safety of your arms.

No stairs, only a ladder: If there are no stairs, ask someone to help you hold your baby while you first get into the pool. Then let them safely hand your child to you. Alternatively, leave your little one on a mat or towel at the side of the pool while you get in. Keep alert and make sure you are never further than an arm's length away from your baby. This way, your child will always be safe.

Once in the Pool

- When you are in the pool, find a good spot and bend your knees until you are shoulder-deep in the water.
- Let your baby feel your presence and allow him to find himself in the new environment and to enjoy the sensation of the water around him.
- Share in your child's experience. Speak calmly with a positive tone of voice and put words to his experience, offering the support he needs.
- When you think your baby is ready for more, you can begin to sway and swing gently together, feeling the water and tuning-in to each other. Move and practice additional activities once comfortable. (Activities can be found starting on page 137.)
- Make sure that your baby is allowed to satisfy his curiosity. Let him look around, taste the water (if he wants to), and feel the sensation of the water against his body. You will be able to watch how your baby takes in the whole experience.
- Gradually, you and your child will feel safer and more and more in sync. At that point, you will be able to move harmoniously in the water together.

Crying and the need for comfort

- If your baby starts crying in the pool, hold her close to you. Don't worry, she is just telling you she needs you more.
- Stay in the comforting, warm water and soothe her as you normally do.
- Shield your child by turning her away from other people or stimuli. It often helps to stay calm and limit her sensory input.
- Once your baby has calmed down and you feel she is ready, gently resume your activities.
- If your child is still upset and her crying increases, get out of the water. Wrap her in a warm towel, soothe her and, if hungry, feed her.
- When your child seems ready again, you can give it another try.

The pacifier can help!

I recommend you bring your baby's pacifier to the pool, if you use one. There is nothing wrong with using it in the water and it can provide comfort. Many times, especially when an experience is new, some children manage easier with their pacifier in their mouths. When your baby becomes familiar with the swimming experience, the pacifier becomes less important and often completely forgotten.

Stop while the swimming is still good

The first few times in the pool are likely to be limited to 10-20 minutes, depending on the age of the baby, your baby's personality, energy level and mood. This may seem like a short amount of time to you, but from your baby's perspective it is a long time and certainly long enough for them to experience what swimming in a pool is all about.

Your little one will have many thoughts during his first visits to the pool. It's not only the act of swimming, but also the new environment, the new experiences in and outside the pool, the smells, the sounds, the noise and the people. It's great to enjoy the experience, and end it on a high note rather than wait for him to be upset and tell you he's done.

After swimming

When the body is wet, you feel cold even if you're in a warm environment. The reason for this is that the body releases heat as water evaporates from the skin. Therefore, it is a good idea to remove your baby's swim suit right after she gets out of the pool and then quickly wrap your little one in a towel that you have standing by.

Baby swimming produces a healthy appetite and a natural fatigue. What your baby needs immediately following class can vary. Some babies want to eat, while others can wait until they have been bathed and dressed. Try to determine what suits your little one best. Even though your child may have slept and eaten before baby swimming, she may need food and a good long nap soon after you're done, too.

If your child is very tired after the swim, then wait and bathe her later. First, let her sleep and if necessary, you can rinse off the chlorine when she has the energy. Normally, delaying a bath won't affect the child's skin. The smell of chlorine may bother you, but it won't bother your child or harm them.

Be aware that it is often very warm inside a swimming facility. Therefore, if the temperature is cold outside then wait to dress your child in too many layers until just before you are leaving the facility, as you want to be careful not to overheat your baby.

Baby swimming offers a lot of stimulation and for your child to take full advantage of the experience, her brain needs time to process all the new sensory information that is coming her way. Because of this, I recommend not planning additional activities on the same day, and instead let swim be the focus of the day, outside of your daily routine.

Swimming Activities

Now, it's finally time to start swimming with your baby! I've grouped activities into three stages.

1. The Beginning: Ways to support your child in the water (page 138)
2. The Next Step: Activities on the water's surface (page 144)
3. Underwater Adventures: Swimming below the water's surface (page 164)

The activities start with basic, introductory activities and progress to more advanced activities, ending with submersion. Babies participating in the first activity group can progress into the second group or straight into Underwater Adventures if your baby feels comfortable and ready for submersions, and then return to the second group. Just continue to do the activities that you and your baby both love to do in the water that introduce and develop new swim activities.

Accompanying each activity is an age recommendation. You'll also find that I have included relational and life skills that each activity promotes.

Keep in mind that the age ranges are only guidelines as every baby will move at their own pace. As you are reviewing, and swimming, you should always be mindful of where your baby is physically, emotionally and cognitively. Pending where you and your child's experience and comfort level are, the activities and pace at which you do them, will vary.

If you try something and it seems like too much, either make the activity less challenging or try again at a different time. If your baby is ready for more, keep going through the activities allowing your baby to explore, practice and develop with you.

When swimming with your baby, keep in mind that your child needs many opportunities to experiment. Make a habit of giving your baby time to try new things. Observe how your child solves problems and encourage him to figure things out on his own. In doing this, you support your child's ability to concentrate, find solutions and develop persistence. All of these are important life skills worth cultivating.

Additionally, remember that practice makes perfect, so make all swim activities interesting and give your little one ample opportunity to keep trying and learning. It may take multiple tries to accomplish a swim activity, but when your baby is ready let her repeat an activity several times, in the same session. Her sense of self-sufficiency will grow and through the process you and she will experience and develop your team-spirit sharing the success.

The Beginning:
Ways to support your child
in the water

The first few times you swim with your baby, it is a good idea to practice the basic ways of supporting your child in the water. Therefore, this first group of activities focuses on a variety of what we call "swimming holds." These are fundamental to learn, with your baby, before progressing to other activities, as it gives a sense of security and comfort for you both in the water.

The various ways you can offer support can feel a bit awkward at first because it is completely different than how you hold your baby on land. You'll learn how to do this, together, and gradually you will feel more comfortable offering your baby support, in a few different ways, as your repertoire expands.

As you grow more adept at supporting your baby in the water, and become more confident in responding to your child's movements, you will also be able to relax more. Once you can relax, you will immediately see the effect it has on your child. Your baby will relax with you and rest comfortably in your hands, as she feels balanced and ready to explore the surroundings with you.

Tummy Time

1. Start with your baby laying on his tummy, resting on your hands.
2. If your baby's neck muscles are not strong enough to hold her head up then bend your wrists so that his chin can rest against your palms, giving him the support he needs.
3. If your child has stronger muscles in her back and neck, and is able to hold her head up, adjust your support by placing your hands under his chest.
4. Lower your shoulders below the surface of the water so that you meet your child at eye level.
5. Move backward in the pool so your child swims forward.
6. When you both feel in sync and balanced, you can vary this support by placing only one hand under your child's chest. By doing this, you are challenging her balance. At the same time, your other hand becomes free allowing you to do something else such as splashing a little on the surface of the water or reaching for a toy that your baby will enjoy.

Allowing a child to swim on her tummy, and offering a little support under her chest, is one of the most common ways to support babies in the water. It is a good starting point for togetherness and interaction, since you are not farther than one arm's length apart. This proximity makes it is easy for you to see and share what captures your child's interest, to make eye contact with him and to enjoy watching your child grow as he takes on a new experience in the world.

This activity promotes: Togetherness, Discovery, Balance

139

Safe Supine

Younger babies often enjoy spending time on their backs in the water. As your child grows older, other things will pique her interest and the reflex to right herself up will emerge. When this development occurs, your child will have difficulty to stay on her back for a long time.

1. Hold your child upright and close to your chest with one of your hands on the back of her head, and the other under her bottom.
2. Lower your child into the water, just as you would lay her on a changing table.
3. Give her time to find her new perspective.
4. When relaxed, gently lower her ears under the water. It often tickles, so talk gently to her and help her relax again.
5. Gently move your arms and hands so your child is lying with her side in front of you.

When you and your child feel safe and relaxed, your hand that supports her under the bottom can be lowered deeper into the water so that she is floating more on her own with you only slightly supporting her head. This is often quite an experience for parents. You will feel amazement and joy the first time you experience your little child floating so well, and your little one will experience a newfound sensation and freedom.

If your child moves, cooperate with her and follow the direction of her swimming. Let her feel the buoyancy in the water, let her linger and enjoy it. You can also encourage her movement by moving backwards. This will form an undercurrent in the water that will lift and "pull" her forward. It will also help keep your child afloat while she senses the water's movement around her body, often resulting in a response in movement.

Perhaps your child will feel most secure when she stays close to you and maintains body contact. If so, you can lean over her and stay close to her. Keep both hands under your child for support. When your child gradually begins to relax, reduce the support and let her feel the buoyancy, while finding balance.

If your child has trouble relaxing when lying on her back, make sure you are not lifting her up too much—or too little—and causing her to feel out of balance or unsupported. She may also need more guidance and support from you, or a longer introduction to this swim hold. Good alternatives can be The Happy Baby Float (page 145) and The Shoulder Float (page 141).

This activity promotes: Trust, Discovery, Delight

Tête-à-Tête—Shoulder Float

Close together, your child rests on your shoulder, cheek to cheek with you, as he floats on his back. It offers a lot of closeness and body contact.

This activity can help your child if it's difficult for him to relax and enjoy lying on his back. It also helps if your child is older and the righting reflex is challenging him in maintaining a horizontal position.

In this hold, your baby will feel support and confidence in you and therefore he will feel that within himself too. If he is tense, help him relax by making adjustments until he is comfortable. Trust, comfort and feeling at ease on the child's back is the goal. When your baby rests comfortably on you, you can take it a step further, by freeing both your hands while you swim, with him floating on you.

1. Stand on the floor of the pool with your child's back towards your chest.
2. Lower your shoulders in the water and lean back a little, guiding your child's head to rest on your shoulder.
3. Let him come close, cheek to cheek.
4. Adjust to his needs—your baby can half-sit or lie face up.
5. Talk, sing a little song or just enjoy the closeness and moment together.

This is a good starting position for a little child, with your support, to become comfortable exploring the sensation of his buoyancy floating on his back. If you make it interesting and comfortable, he will learn to enjoy it.

This activity promotes: Trust, Togetherness, Delight

141

The Sandwich with a Twist

This is a good activity when you support your child in a twist from his tummy to his back and vice versa.

1. Start in Tummy Time and move one of your hands right under your child so she rests her chest on this hand.
2. When you feel that she is well supported, and you have balance, move the other hand and place it on your child's back for balance and support. Voilà, you have a little baby sandwich!
3. Your fingers are pointing down toward your child's legs as you lower yourself into the water, with your shoulders under the water's surface so you can meet in eye level with your baby.
4. Invite your child to do the twist with you.
5. Slowly let your baby twist from his tummy to his back with your help. The arm with the hand that rests on your child's back supports your child's head throughout the twist.
6. Follow with the movement. While you twist him around, you come to a standing position, making eye-contact easy.
7. When your child is finally on his back, stand so that your baby is right in front of you and he easily can look up and see you.
8. If your child feels safe and relaxed, the hand on the tummy can be moved away or used to help move your other hand from his back to the back of his head.
9. You support your child under the head or under the shoulder blades. By supporting under the shoulder blades, his head is free and he gets more sensory stimulation.

Throughout the twist, allow your child to have eye contact with you. By doing this calmly and with good support, he can remain balanced. When standing behind your child, lean over him and if he isn't already looking at you, see if you can get his attention. When he looks up at you, you will notice how his body position becomes horizontal and more balanced in the water. This position allows him to enjoy freedom in his movements and lets both of you explore buoyancy.

Once your child knows how to twist from his back to his tummy (and possibly also from the tummy to the back) and to initiate a twist, follow his lead and join in on his learning. Your hands simply follow the movements of your child and provide the necessary support. Practicing this twist naturally can support your child's ability to independently swim longer stretches later on.

Your child learns to swim, rotate, and catch a breath while resting on his back before rotating back onto his tummy and continuing to swim. Later, this rotation will become freestyle breathing.

This activity promotes: Leadership, Connection, Cooperation

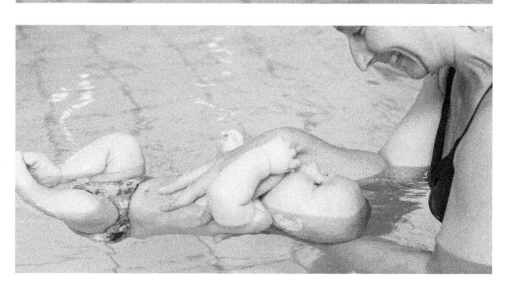

Activities on the surface

The following activities focus on swimming on the surface of the water while incorporating elements that contribute to learning and development. The activities range from supportive swim holds to those that promote cooperation and teamwork. As your child becomes a stronger person (physically and emotionally), they also become a stronger swimmer, with your help.

This section of activities will help you explore how to pique and sustain your child's interest. It will also help you find the appropriate swim challenges for your child and determine how to best guide your baby's progress toward independence.

Through swimming, you will give your little one rich opportunities to develop her sensory systems and motor skills, along with her emotional and social skills. Through teamwork, and your child's drive and persistence to practice learning, you'll further develop and build-up the foundation for resilience using these swim activities.

Happy Baby Float

1. Let your child rest her back on the inside of your forearms with her legs up against your chest.
2. Allow her head to rest in your cupped palms.
3. Here you can rock her gently from side to side in the water.

This is a good position for your child when she is still small, in need of a rest, and/or is simply in the mood to be close to you and cuddle. This position allows for plenty of body and eye contact, along with a little conversation. This position is also a good alternative for a child who needs more support in order to become comfortable on her back.

This activity promotes: Connection, Delight, Comfort

From 3-4 months

Swing Time

1. Lower yourself so that you and your baby are both chest-deep in the water, facing each other, with you supporting your child under his arms.
2. Open your hands so that your child is hanging with his armpits between your thumbs and index fingers.
3. Stand with one leg in front of the other and start moving back and forth.
4. Let your child join you in the swinging, while you increase the swing with your arms and make adjustments to create a pleasant rhythmic feeling.

Pay attention to the resistance of the water and work with it. You can extend the movement for your child by gently pressing your fingers on his shoulder blades and letting him move onto his back. When he swings back, gently press with your thumbs so that he rotates all the way over onto his tummy, almost into the Tummy Time position (see page 139).

Create a pleasant swinging motion. Maintain good contact and enhance the experience with facial expressions that will make your child bubble over with joy.

This activity promotes: Connection, Joy & Delight, Multiple Sensory Input

Floating (almost) independently

If your child is comfortable on his back and if you feel confident engaging in a trusting collaboration, your child may be able to learn to float (almost) independently on her back. You can help her do this by gradually reducing your physical support, while showing her great emotional support through your positive attention, eye contact, and encouragement. This will show your baby you trust in her ability to accomplish this activity on her own, and at the same time that she can always trust that you will be there when she needs you!

1. Support your child's head as she lies on her back.
2. Make sure you have good eye contact and also that she is very comfortable in this position.
3. Gradually reduce your support, first by just giving support with your fingers and then taking away one finger at a time, always in cooperation with your child, making sure that she is balanced, focused, and actively participating.
4. If you find that your child is floating on her own then slowly let your hands float out to the sides. Keep in mind that any movement will cause the water to shift, which could easily make your child lose her balance, so remember to move gently.
5. Stay present and alert to her needs.

This activity promotes: Trust, Connection, Buoyancy

147

A Word of Warning!

There are swim programs around the world advertising and showing infants who can lie and float by themselves for several consecutive minutes. Babies who can do this have been trained in self-rescue techniques, which rely on severe backfloating and submersion tactics, and putting the child into stressful situations to get them to perform a task.

I am not an expert in these methods, but after more than 25 years actively researching the subject and working directly with babies and parents, I believe these methods can be harmful. I strongly discourage parents from using these courses. In many cases, parents enroll their children in self-rescue courses because they are terrified that their children will drown.

As parents it is natural to be worried your child will come into danger or be hurt, but the cost of learning this skill, in this way, is far too high, and here's why: self-rescue methods go against the strong instincts your baby was born with for seeking and needing the feeling of trust and protection from their caregiver. Basically, these methods teach your baby to seek something other than you for trust and protection.

These methods deliberately, and repeatedly, put a child into a stressful situation, neglect the cries from the child and, from what we know from research today, can induce developmental trauma. The child becomes stressed to a degree that is far beyond what is healthy for a small baby's sensitive stress system and malleable brain. The consequences can be profound and last long into the future.

Never let a program, or teacher, suggest a method that feels odd or numbs your empathy. Your instincts allow you to meet your child's needs of asking for help if he is feeling stressed. It's not our children's responsibility to keep themselves safe—it's ours! Your baby naturally trusts that you are taking full responsibility for his safety. See links (page 196-197) for organizations working for awareness about risk of drowning and layers of protection.

From 3-4 months

The Kitesurfer

It can never be too early to start kitesurfing! When your child is 3-4 months, and can hold her head up, she will find it quite wonderful to lie on her back and surf across the water's surface while enjoying the sensation of speed, with you by her side.

1. Stand so that you can keep your balance, and let one thigh act as a platform on which your child can rest her back.
2. Hold out your thumbs for your little one to hold on to, and place the rest of your fingers on the back of your child's hand.
3. Make eye contact and when ready, lower your thigh—"the platform"—gently into the water, and let your child float while she is holding onto your fingers.
4. Give her a gentle "surf" on the surface of the water.

When the child grows older, and becomes stronger in her neck and back muscles, the horizontal position will be replaced by a more vertical position which will allow her to swing back and forth through the water, with your help.

For a baby younger than six months, the gripping reflex is still present. Your baby might have a tight hold on your fingers, but you cannot fully rely on the stability of her grip. For this reason, it's a good idea to gently hold onto the back of her hand with your fingers ready to take a stronger hold if her grip loosens.

When your child holds a conscious grip, and is comfortable submerging, you can expand the activity by letting her hold on by herself. This gives her the opportunity to learn how firmly she should hold onto you, and teaches her to maintain the hold. It also gives her the freedom to let go, submerge into the water and swim to you, or rest when she needs wants to, providing independence.

This activity promotes: Communication, Cooperation, Multiple Sensory Input, Emotional Development

Balancing Ring

There are many kinds of swim rings. The ring I am referencing here is a small, special inflatable swim ring for baby swimmers that has an inner diameter of approximately 7 to 7.5 inches (18-19 cm). It purposely does not have a seat so that the baby, in cooperation with the parent or caregiver, can learn how to balance, propel and change directions in the water herself. For this reason, I have renamed the swim ring to the "balancing ring" to distinguish it from a passive floatation device.

Balancing is a fun activity. You give your child the support she needs and gradually let her take over until she can balance in it on her own.

1. Let your child rest her back against your chest and hold your arm around her chest.
2. Gather her feet together, with your free hand, and lower her into the ring.
3. Let your child's chest rest on the front of the ring. Her arms can extend out to each side.
4. The entire ring should be floating on the water.
5. Offer your child light support. If she leans too far forward, you can place one of your fingers under the ring.

While supporting her, make sure that you have "dynamic hands," which means you follow the movements in the water and your child can feel the effects that the water has. The goal is for your child to find, and keep, her balance in the ring. As soon as she is able to do this, it is a real pleasure to watch her propel herself through the water. You'll be pleasantly struck by your child's satisfaction and sense of freedom.

This activity promotes: Cooperation, Balance, Joy

Word of Advice

Any flotation device can end up being a disservice if used too much because it can become a crutch that prevents them from learning the intended skill. Moderation is key, so that your child feels supported, but also experiences what it really feels like to learn how to float and swim without an aid. With the balancing ring, it is a great tool to use for a short period of time for your baby to experience some freedom, but it should be used with other activities as well to ensure she is learning.

As a side note, in the beginning, getting your baby out of the ring can be a challenge. Here is one way to keep your child comfortable as you do this:

1. Let your child rest her head on your shoulder as you slide one arm around her chest.
2. Lean back and push the balancing ring into the water while pulling the ring over the child's legs. The water helps reduce friction and the only thing you need to pull on is the balancing ring.

The Carousel

The Carousel is a very good way to support your child when he can hold his head up. Once your activities in the water are well underway, he will swim around and explore his surroundings, claiming an ever larger radius and view, with you next to him sharing in the adventure.

1. Place your child on his tummy and let his chest rest on your extended forearm. For extra support, you can hold him gently around his distant upper arm.

2. Position yourself so that you are at eye level with your child. This allows you to observe what catches his attention and to easily make eye contact, when needed, for extra comfort and emotional support.

From 4-5 months

The Scout

In this hold, your little one lies on her tummy with the support from your hands around her chest. From this position, she will be able to see more of her surroundings. You will be right next to her so that you can see what captures her interest. In cooperation with your child, you can help her swim toward the object of her interest.

1. With your child lying on her tummy, stand next to her and support her around the chest with both hands.
2. Drop down so you are in eye-level with your child.
3. Feel the buoyancy of the water and find the level at which your child is suspended primarily by the water. Support as much (or as little) as is needed so that she can easily lie with her head above the surface of the water.
4. Your child can now look forward to freely move in that direction, as well as from side to side. Cooperate with her, so her movements will take her forward through the water.
5. Hold your baby with a light touch so she is able to experience the water influencing her motions.

Some children just lie back in this hold, not wanting to move. A toy can sometimes spark interest to get her moving, but tune-in and play around with what works best for your little one.

Pro tip: From the ages of 8-10 months (give or take) a baby will respond to toys that sink, as her awareness and attention is growing. When a baby notices and follows the toys sinking to the bottom of the pool, it will arouse her interest. Retrieving the toy is challenging, and it can be hard to estimate the distance through the water. Your little diver maybe need to take breaks to the surface of the water, but once the child's interest has been sparked, she will work on problem-solving and keep trying until she succeeds (maybe with a little help from you). Once she's figured it out, the activity will likely continue into deeper waters.

This activity promotes: Cooperation, Interest, Focus

153

Pool Noodles

A Pool Noodle is another flotation device that can be used in a variety of ways. It's use in the water is only limited by your imagination. Some children need a slow introduction to it, while others embrace its possibilities right away. Your child will learn ways of how to use it, in collaboration with you. Here are three ways I like to use Pool Noodles:

Option 1: Your child has his arms over the noodle. You position yourself in front of him and support him gently under the noodle, so he feels the water and can find his balance. Keep an eye on where he is swimming, encourage his movements and let him enjoy the feeling of freedom.

Option 2: Use two noodles floating parallel to each other. Place yourself and your baby in between the two noodles. Position your baby so she is facing you, and place a noodle under each of her arms. Face your baby, and place one noodle under each of your arms. Now that both of you have one noodle under both of your arms, you can swim together.

When you and your child become more adept at using Pool Noodles, you can let your baby swim forward, with you behind her, as you both glide with her leading the way.

Option 3: Use the pool noodle simply to relax and connect with your baby. Put a noodle behind your neck and under your arms. Then lie on your back with your baby on your tummy. Simply float around and enjoy life close together.

This activity promotes: Cooperation, Balance, Joy

Piggyback

It can be fun for your child to piggyback, on you, while you swim. This is also a good collaborative activity for your child to learn how to hold onto you.

1. Lift up your knee and let your child sit on it, facing you.
2. Cross your arms and hold hands with your child.
3. Lower yourself down so your shoulders are in the water.
4. Gently swing your little one around onto your back. Let him stay as low as possible, in the water, as the water helps reduce weight and creates less friction.
5. The first few times you do this activity, hold gently onto your child's hands as you walk, or gently jump, around in the water.

When you and your child are comfortable in this activity, guide him to hold onto your neck or shoulders by himself. When he does, you can swim.

Once your child feels comfortable on your back, you can expand this activity to include a tandem submersion. Make sure you communicate clearly before you dip under so your baby knows what to expect.

What a thrill! And when your little "Piggybacker" can talk, you'll hopefully hear enthusiastic calls for "Again!", "More!", "Faster, faster!"

This activity promotes: Exploring, Comfort, Joy, Closeness

From 5-6 months

Carousel Ride

Make *The Carousel* into a Carousel Ride by adding a little more speed and movement.

1. Start by supporting your child in The Carousel (see page 152).
2. Stand with your legs spread slightly apart on the floor of the pool.
3. Tighten your abdominal muscles and turn around in a circle in the same direction as your child is looking.
4. Keep a pace that is appropriate for your child and occasionally take a break to make eye contact and tune-in with him, and share the experience.

Some parents may find it difficult to support their child in this way. If your baby feels too heavy, place one of your hands under his hips and support him with both of your hands.

The movement and response of the water often triggers a desire in the child to move and kick his legs. This is a wonderful interactive activity that allows you to share your child's focus, experience something together and be playful by picking up speed in the water.

This activity promotes: Joy, Cooperation, Emotional Development

The Royal Rocker

For this hold, your child can simply sit and rest her back against your chest, whether she is playing with a toy or just relaxing. You can also gently bounce and sway, while she is reclined on you. The Royal Rocker is also the starting point for The Royal Launch (see page 174).

1. Let your child sit on your hands with her back leaning against your chest.
2. Lower down or adjust so she sits chest deep in the water.
3. Make sure your child is sitting comfortably and can relax.

This activity promotes: Togetherness, Comfort, Joy

From 5-6 months

Climbing up onto the Deck

Holding onto the wall and then climbing out of the pool independently are two milestones in baby swim. These activities lead to a feeling of self-sufficiency. These skills also help you and your child in reaching a bigger goal of baby swim—jumping into the pool and then repeating the process of finding the wall and crawling out of the pool to do it again... and again!

Around the time your child begins to crawl on land, he may also start to crawl up from the pool to the pool deck. Support your baby by being by his side, while he begins to explore the wall and allow him to practice this, with you helping.

1. Let your child hold onto the wall of the pool.
2. If needed, gently support your child under his bottom.
3. Watch your child closely and offer support as needed. For example, he may need some guidance in lifting up the first leg as he starts to climb out.

If your little one loses interest, it could be because it's too difficult or that the activity doesn't have meaning for him, yet. If this occurs, I recommend you give him encouragement and a little extra support by putting an exciting toy on the deck, just beyond his reach, prompting his response to want to retrieve it.

This activity promotes: Independence, Sensory Stimulation, Motor-development, Confidence

From 5-6 months

Swim to the Wall

This activity helps your child form an important habit in swimming. Every time she jumps to you from the pool deck, make sure that you help her finish the activity by returning to the wall, taking hold of it and possibly even climbing up onto the pool deck, again. Being able to do this will depend on your baby's age and motor skills, as well as her strength.

Once your child is familiar with this routine and she reaches for the wall on her own, you can take the next step and let her learn to gradually swim independently back to the wall, after she jumps into the water.

1. Start with your child on her tummy and you supporting her under her arms like in The Scout (see page 153).
2. Stand so that you can easily make eye contact with her.
3. Make sure that you have both identified your common target, such as the pool wall, approximately 2 to 4 feet away.
4. When your child is ready, communicate as you usually do, for example, "One, two, three, go!"
5. Let her swim towards the wall at her pace, and help her when and if she needs it.
6. In the beginning, gently support your baby while she swims to the wall and gradually encourage her to swim on her own.

7. Once she reaches the wall, allow your child to hold onto it so she becomes familiar with the feeling of the wall (texture, temperature, etc.). If your child tries to climb up then support her effort and guide her.

As she gains more experience, she will deliberately head toward the wall after plunging from the deck. Once she does this, you can let her alternate between this activity and taking a Royal Launch (page 174).

Initially, your child will swim a short distance. Gradually, together with you, she will develop the ability to swim longer distances.

Swimming to the wall is one of the interim skills that your child learns on her path to more independence, as it gives her the ability to reach and grab the wall. Throughout this process, the collaboration between you and your child is key.

This activity promotes: Challenge, Cooperation, Confidence, Independence

Swimming Legs

A good kick in the water, which I like to call "swimming legs" is very important for effective forward propulsion in the water. The way we move our legs in the water differs from how we walk or run on land, so every child needs to develop their swimming legs.

There is a simple way to help your child start developing strong swimming legs early on. Initially, your child will use the same patterns of movement in water as on land, but this isn't very effective in the water. A kick is most effective in the water when both legs are extended, the feet are relaxed (but not limp) and the big toes almost touch each other when they pass each other in the kicking motion. This is the starting point for an effective kick and great swimming legs.

Here is one way to practice:

1. Let your child lie on her tummy, or on her back, with her head resting on your shoulder while you are leaning back.
2. Gently wrap your hands around your child's knees.
3. Make soft and rhythmic kicking movements, allowing your child's big toes to brush up against each other whenever her feet meet in the middle.
4. Say "kick, kick, kick," wait for a reaction and see if your child starts kicking on her own.
5. Repeat and make it a fun game for your child. This activity involves a collaboration for which you act as your child's guide.

Time the kicking movements in the water just before your child takes off on an independent swim (for example, if your child is swimming towards the wall), as this will help her remember how to use her strong swimming legs. A baby will need a lot of repetition, so make practicing fun and nurture her interest in this activity. With time, kicking will become automatic and your child will discover that quality kicking is the key to getting around efficiently in the water, as she learns to swim. Similar to riding a bike, once your child learns her swimming legs, she will never forget.

This activity promotes: Guiding, Interest, Focus

From 5-6 months

The Trampoline

For this activity, support your baby by gently holding her hips. Your child is challenged to use her upper body to balance herself.

1. Gently lay your child down in the water on her back the same way you would lay her onto a changing table.
2. Support her with one hand under her head and your other hand under her bottom.
3. When you see that she is comfortable, and you have a good grasp of her, move the hand that was supporting her bottom and take a light hold of one hip.
4. In cooperation with her, gently lower the hand that her head was resting on a little deeper into the water. Your child should respond by tensing up the muscles in her core and neck, finding new balance and floating.
5. Carefully move the hand that's under your child's head down so that it now wraps around her other hip.
6. Be sure to maintain good contact with your child at all times.

You can release this position in two different ways.

Option 1: The quick and easy way to release your child is to move one hand from your child's hip, place it under her head, and lift your child up the same way you laid her down.

Option 2: The more advanced way is to calmly, and easily, push your child's hips down in the water until she is sitting or standing in a vertical position. The shoulders of the child should remain in the water, as you want to ensure you do not put strain on the baby's spine.

Caution: Supporting your baby this way may trigger a reflex that causes your child to arch backward into the water. If you do not catch this action, it will cause water to enter your baby's nose, which is harmless, but can be a very unpleasant sensation that you should try to prevent. This can be avoided by maintaining good contact and being present and alert of all movements with your baby. Should your child arch back, avoid pulling her out of the water and showing fear. Help her move calmly, but quickly, into a vertical position. Follow your child's reaction and answer her needs. Your child will likely be surprised and begin to cough if she has water up her nose and she might need some time in your comforting arms before she is ready for new adventures again that day.

This activity promotes: Leadership, Readiness, Responsiveness

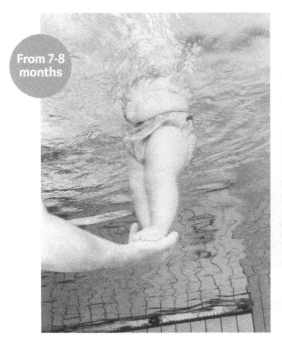

Balance Tower

A child has fun when his balancing skills are engaged and challenged, as long as the task does not exceed what he can manage. In the water, balance is naturally promoted in many different ways. The Balance Tower is a collaborative activity with an exciting challenge for both the adult and the child. In this activity, your child balances on your hand and you make it fun for both of you.

1. Let your child sit on your knee and face you.
2. Place one hand under his arm as you gather both his feet together with your other hand.
3. Once you achieve a good grip (without squeezing your child's feet), lift him up and allow him to stand in your hand.

For this activity, the two of you balance together, maintaining adequate contact and sharing the experience.

It is easier for you and your child to keep his balance when he is surrounded by water. As you lift him up and out of the water, it challenges both of you to balance better and build strength.

Some children have "spaghetti legs," meaning that during every attempt to help them stand, they sit back down. If this happens, try to help your child by making it clear that he is standing on a solid foundation (e.g., your hand). If this doesn't work, just let your child sit and balance in your hand. The two of you can always return to the standing variation later. In the meantime, you can have fun with the sitting version and enjoy the experience together!

This activity promotes: Leadership, Balance, Joy, Cooperation, Empathy

Walking in Water

It's both exciting and challenging for your child to walk around and stand by himself on the pool floor. The buoyancy of the water makes balancing, and moving in the water, more challenging and easier said than done.

Your child may be a little cautious and that is because he is smart and might already have felt that this activity needs more attention. Gradually, he will become more sure of his footing. Let him explore what it feels like to stand, walk, run and jump in the water with you by his side. If your child loses his balance when the speed increases, gently guide him back up to the surface of the water or over to the wall. After guiding him a couple of times, you will notice how he will start to make these movements on his own.

By standing on the pool floor or on the stairs, your child can eventually learn how to launch from there and then swim to you, and your waiting hands, in deeper waters.

This activity will allow your child to experience buoyancy, develop good balance and practice launching. You will share his happiness as you watch your little explorer walk around joyfully in the water beside you.

This activity promotes: Safe and Secure, Attention, Balance, Buoyancy

The Underwater Adventure

Once you and your child are ready, the adventure can continue underwater! In this final section of activities, I'll share all the opportunities that will open up for you and your child in this advanced baby swimming activity guide. Before diving under it's very important that you and your baby feel ready. You'll know you're both ready when you feel comfortable in the water, with basic swimming techniques outlined in activity sections 1 and 2, and have built up strength—physically, emotionally and cognitively.

Underwater Activities

The guidance in Part 1 of this book and the activities listed so far in Part 2 have provided a foundation of physical knowledge. More importantly, I hope I have communicated the importance of focusing on your empathy, trust and comfort so that you and your baby can attempt these underwater activities with confidence.

Children like to discover the possibilities in their world, and for a small baby swimmer, exploring the underwater world is a natural next step. When she has built her abilities in submerging, she will be able to swim around more independently and develop her swimming skills together with you. This will parallel her development on land.

Before you submerge with your baby for the first time, make sure you are both ready. Being comfortable in the water has meaning to your baby, so keep this in mind, as well as your baby's desire to be independent in the water—similar to his actions on land. In the water, more cooperation is needed, but the concept of guiding your baby and keeping him safe remains the same as any other activity. Pay attention to when your baby is reaching out for opportunities and go with those cues. It is quite astonishing and truly a pleasure to see how even small babies can self-assuredly make their way through the water.

When young children submerge, they use a protective reflex that prevents water from entering their respiratory tract. However, your child should quickly learn to hold her breath deliberately instead of by reflex. Your child will either learn to do this on her own or as a result of interacting, and practicing, with you while you make it easy for her to follow your lead. When your child starts to consciously, deliberately hold her breath, she will do so by closing the airways in her throat in the same way that advanced swimmers do. This technique is natural, easy, and a much more appropriate method as opposed to closing the mouth and holding the nose, as many have learned.

Submerging should be a natural part of being in water, never forced. It is important that it makes sense for your child. Once your child feels comfortable both above and below the water's surface, great opportunities for further discovery and exploration will be available to him. This helps your child develop a sense of security and confidence early on. Even when children feel comfortable and secure around water, remember that it is always your responsibility to keep them safe. Children do not have the capacity to judge whether or not a situation is sufficiently safe, or to predict consequences, so stay with your child at all times.

Many people also wonder about the "diving reflex," also known as the "diving response protective reflex." This protective reflex prevents water from entering our airway. While this does protect us, it is not a fail-safe and your baby being ready to go underwater remains to be of the most important. When a child shows they are ready and you react by guiding them through the underwater adventure, the mutual love of swimming, and each other, will deepen.

Ready to explore the underwater world?

When you and your child both feel comfortable in the water, you are likely ready to also explore the world underwater. Ask yourself whether your child is prepared and eager for new and slightly more challenging swim experiences. One indicator will be that she splashes in the water and moves in a relaxed way. You can also tell that she is ready to submerge when she is comfortable and relaxed getting water on her face. It might also be the case that she has already submerged on her own, in which case these activities, in the pages to follow, are a natural next step to take with your baby.

Why submerge?

Many parents understandably have mixed feelings about submerging their child. They simultaneously feel excitement, worry and discomfort. Pausing to consider why you will, or will not, submerge with your child is important. It's necessary that you, as a parent, become clear about what you want, because you emotionally affect your child. If you are comfortable, then this message will reach your child. If you are unsure, scared or skeptical, but submerge with the child anyway, then the mixed message may create confusion and insecurity in your child, too.

In order to prepare, you can ask yourself the question, "Do I want to submerge my child?". If you are unsure, I recommend you wait, as you have plenty of time to do this together later. If you would like to submerge together with your baby, think about the experience you want to give your child in this adventure. Thinking it through before hand makes it much easier to gain control over your own feelings, and to focus on your child's experience, so that you can help ensure all goes well.

When and how you start to submerge will vary. Some parents start early on, guiding the submerging with clear, easy to follow communication. Others wait for their child to take the initiative. If you choose to not submerge with your child, I would remind you not to prevent your child from trying to do so if they are curious. Always tune-in to your baby and be mindful of the cues your child is giving you.

Just as on land, your child will investigate and interact with the water environment as she swims early on. In the water, it is natural for your baby to explore the surface, the boundary between air and water, and also to go underwater. At first, this will happen randomly, and then over time it will become more and more conscious. Encourage your child's curiosity and desire to learn. Alternatively, if you prevent your baby from trying and learning, it may halt the discovery process all together.

When children learn to submerge through verbal prompts, the adult acts as the initiator. Make sure to maintain equality with your child. Pay close attention to her and if she shows signs of not wanting to go under then you should stop. If she is ready, keep going. Work as a team and allow your baby to maintain an active role in her swimming adventure.

If you enroll in a group class, the instructor will probably introduce you to submerging at some point. Sometimes this happens during the first lesson, which I think is too soon for both of you. Why rush? In other cases, submerging isn't introduced until much later, possibly as part of an advanced course. My recommendation is that you tune-in and go with your child's readiness and desire to explore. You may or may not time things correctly, but every child is different and ultimately you are the one who knows your child best. If you misjudge things along the way, take responsibility, and restore trust in your baby. Again, babies are quick to forgive and as the primary person you will always be the person with whom your child feels safest.

How often and how deep should we submerge?

Submerging for the first time is often an incredible experience for parents and a moment of surprise for the child. I suggest doing it early in the lesson, or when you first enter the pool (if alone), but without feeling rushed. The best way is to time it so that your child has energy and enthusiasm, but has gained his swim legs too and knows exactly where he is.

Submersion is always just underneath the water's surface. The idea of it, is that it leads to swimming freely, so you want to ensure the depth is where you'd have your baby if he were swimming on his own.

One way I recommend introducing submersions is to use the same, clear communications before each submersion. For example, communicate using mimicry and clear verbal signals such as, "One, two, three!" or "Ready? Go!" By using the same communications repeatedly, your child will learn by his own experience and by following your lead. You want him to be able to eventually understand your communication, participate actively and also become in control so he can submerge freely, versus using a reflex. Once your child recognizes the pattern and learns to submerge, he will prepare and close his airways by his own will.

I recommend you give your baby three successive, gentle and short submersions, with short breaks in between, to initiate eye contact and assess how they are doing. Never rush. What is important is your child's reaction and your response to it. Focus on how you invite your child into the water. Maintain good contact with him and make it easy for him to understand you are leading him into the activity so he knows to follow you.

The first time under the water will be a surprise for your child, but by the third time some children will already recognize the pattern and prepare for their next dip under. The more your child has experienced clear and responsive communication and guiding from you the easier it becomes for him to learn it.

When your child submerges, his body should never be tense and he should never look afraid. If you notice either of these signs then your child is not yet ready to be submerging.

After introducing submersions, the number of dips down under the water can be extended by one or two each lesson. As long as your child is up for it, submersions are okay with a maximum of seven per pool session.

The amount of times you choose to submerge each lesson is also important for finding the balance between teaching your baby how to do it and enjoying it. For example, if you choose to submerge only one or two times per lesson, and there is a week before swimming again, your child may not have enough time to practice and retain the ability properly. This may cause your baby to dislike the experience all together. On the flip side, if you repeat the process too many times in one session, it can become overwhelming and exhaust your child. Look at your child, read his signals and decide what's best for your little one. Submerging must never be a struggle for your child, but rather one of many swim skills that he will acquire and enjoy.

Remember that your bond of trust is the most important thing. Trust is the emotional footprint that matters most and has a lasting effect in the bigger picture. You are also nurturing your baby's self-esteem and inner drive by having a dialogue. Your baby begins to understand they have a choice and can communicate (with or without words). Your baby also understand that his needs are being listened to and respected by you.

The activity of submerging should leave you and your child with positive feelings. If you feel anything else, wait before trying again, and proceed slowly next time.

Important Note: Prolonged apnea
Prolonged apnea (an unusually long interruption in breathing) after submerging rarely occurs when the activity has been introduced gently and comfortably. That said, if you notice your child takes 10 to 15 seconds to resume breathing after submerging, it is essential to keep calm so that any fear he may have does not intensify—that could delay resumption of breathing even longer. The cause of this condition is not known, but we do know that there's an increased risk of it in children who have had upper respiratory tract infections or who are pressured into submerging.

How do you submerge with the child?

There are many ways to submerge with your child, but the approach I teach focuses on communication, awareness and collaboration. It is an easy and more natural model to use for this activity.

Submerge with Verbal and Physical Communication

1. Your child is lying on her tummy, resting on your hands.
2. Get your child's attention and make eye contact.
3. Communicate using mimicry and clear verbal signals (i.e., "One, two, three, go!" or "Ready? Go!")
4. Lift up your child a little bit while you inhale audibly. (The lift will be the physical signal and the moment during which your child will eventually prepare herself to submerge.)
5. Lower your child gently below the surface of the water.
6. After a short swim, glide her back up through the water until she is above the surface again.
7. When your child returns, she will reflect for a brief moment before she is ready to reconnect with you and look for feedback.
8. Tune-in and respond to her experience and expression. You may say something like, "Hi! You swam underwater! How was it?" "That was new! You seemed to liked it! Are you OK?" or "You got surprised, was that a little too much for you right now? I'm sorry, but I promise you're okay. I'm right here...".

This activity promotes: Leadership, Communication, Trust, Responsiveness

Make sure your support is positive

If you are nervous, your baby may sense this as you hold him. Too tight of a grip signals that you are nervous and that something unpleasant might be happening. If you are frightened, you'll likely show the concern on your face and your baby will see it when they look at you after they come back from being submerged. Remember that your child learns from experience and if your grip is tight and uncomfortable, and the look he sees on your face signals fear, then he will associate this activity with fear and worry. It's completely okay to be nervous, but do your best to keep your emotions in check so you are not imprinting unnecessary negative feelings onto your child. Again, being submerged is a natural part of swimming, so once you and your baby are ready, it will be a positive and good experience for both of you.

A note about crying

Children who are ready to submerge don't cry. If your child is crying, he is communicating that something is wrong and that he needs your help.

Respond and help him find his calm again. Try to find an explanation for why he is upset. It can be that the activity was done too soon, too fast, done for too long, or because he wasn't in the right mood. Most of the time there is something you can easily do to help him feel better. For example, you can be more clear in explaining what is going to happen, shorten the time he is under the water, make the movement more gentle, and/or give him more time to be able to follow you better through the activity.

In some cases, it's also because it's too soon to submerge. In this case, the solution is to take a break from submerging and resume when your child is better prepared, and ready, for the underwater experience.

Should I blow in my baby's face before submerging?
Many parents ask if they should blow air in a child's face before submerging because they have heard that many people do this. The answer is no, blowing in your child's face before going under the water is not necessary.

Blowing activates the facial reflex which causes your baby to hold his breath before he goes underwater. Perhaps you've noticed that your baby holds his breath while being outside when the wind blows. Many swim schools of the past generations (and some swim schools today) taught this technique, but I recommend a more gentle approach for submerging focused on open communication and guiding your child. With the model I am teaching you, your child can keep control over his own breath, which gives him a sense of self-reliance and respects his pace. Again, if your baby isn't ready, then simply wait and try again another time. Resist forcing the submersion activity with "tricks" like blowing in a baby's face.

After you and your baby have mastered the basics of submerging

When submerging feels natural, and you feel you and your baby have a good communication with mutual understanding, you and your child may be ready for more activities.

The next step is to work together to naturally extend your child's swim skills so that he is given the opportunity to learn to swim for longer distances and stretches of time. The following pages cover activities to help reach these milestones.

Progression of submerging

Submersion is a skill that needs to be cultivated, over time, with lots of practice.

As your baby builds confidence, she will want to stretch her abilities so help her gradually lengthen both her time in the pool and her swimming distance. Submersion is the first step to independent swimming. As you and your child develop your swimming skills, always maintain your communication and stay tuned-in. Team-work is key!

From 3-4 months

Your Child's First Independent Swim to You

Because children progress to independent swimming gradually, and every child has a different experience, if you have multiple children, you can expect different timeframes and responses from each child as they learn to swim.

As it relates to independent swim, the experience of letting go of your child in the water will allow her to feel her balance in the water and make her first little swims. You will have the experience of following along and seeing your child achieve this significant milestone. You will start gently, of course, and remain right there with her for her security and guidance.

1. Get your baby's attention and communicate with her. If you and your baby are in sync get ready to go under the water: "One, two, three, go!"

2. Lift your child up and let her slide down under the water, again.
3. While doing this, lean back.
4. Gently release your child, helping her stay balanced, while your arms float to the side.
5. Let your baby swim to your chest or shoulders and resurface there. If she is not swimming herself, give her a little support and guide her into your chest and up out of the water.

This may seem like a short distance, but it's a major accomplishment for you and your baby! Once complete, you should celebrate together with smiles, hugs and kisses. The confidence you will each gain with this activity is huge and will lead to progression in other abilities in the water.

This activity promotes: Trust, Leadership, Confidence, Resilience

From 5-6 months

The Free Swim

The free swim is many families' favorite activity, as it requires three people. This is your child's first independent swim from one adult to another. It is a nice activity involving cooperation between everyone involved.

1. Let your child swim to the adult he is most comfortable with (Adult A), as this helps set the tone and comfort level for the baby. This means the other parent or guardian (Adult B) should be holding the baby to begin this activity.
2. You (Adult A) stand about two to three feet away, facing your child, and the other adult (Adult B) is holding the child.
3. Your child is on his tummy gently supported in The Scout (page 153) by Adult B.
4. When ready, Adult A will call on the child's attention and communicate that it is time to go under the water. For example, say, "Are you ready?" If you seem to be in sync with your baby, say, "One, two, three, go!"
5. In a coordinated sliding motion, Adult B lifts the child up a little before he slides down, in the natural swimming position just below the surface of the water.

6. If the child is balanced then Adult B gently releases their hands out to the side.
7. The child swims through the water toward Adult A.
8. Adult A forms her hands into a plate under the baby's chest where he can comfortably land and meet you.
9. Meet and greet each other with joy and encouragement!
10. Continue in the Tummy Time (page 139), unless your child needs to come up for a cuddle.

When releasing the child into his independent swim, move calmly because too much movement causes turbulence in the water, which can make it more difficult for your child to maintain his balance. If your child doesn't move much, then step in and meet him. Never push a child in the water because they will expect to be pushed and not learn to propel themselves, which is a crucial part of swimming.

This activity promotes: Trust, Confidence, Resilience

174

The Royal Launch

Underwater activities are such a fun adventure to do with your child! Parents and other guardians, extended family members, and friends, all love swimming with babies when the underwater adventure is present. Babies love the support, trust and confidence they are building with their favorite people around them, cheering them on, and playing with them.

In this next activity your child swims toward a target such as a person, the wall, the stairs or a toy. The activity has the same starting position as The Royal Rocker (page 157).

1. Start by making sure you and your child know the target you want to swim towards.
2. Let your child sit on the palm of your hands so that she can lean her back against your chest.
3. Once you have indicated that it is okay to swim, and your little one decides to push off, follow her movement forward while allowing her to lean away from your chest as she swims toward the target you've selected together.
4. In cooperation with your child, refine the timing of the jump-off and the smoothness of the landing in order to achieve a shared feeling of success.

Be mindful and gentle of not creating extra turbulence in the water that could disrupt your baby's balance. The baby's own gentle push-off, combined with your help getting her to maintain her balance, will give her the best shot of swimming to the target.

In this activity you collaborate with your child and you will experience how you gradually learn how to balance better together. Soon your child will become a more experienced swimmer. She will swim with balance, confidence and orient herself under the water while swimming to her goal.

If your child does not want to launch, it may either be that the distance is too far or that your child is not interested in this activity at that moment. Your child's hesitation will be obvious because she will continue to lean back against your chest. Try to determine the source of your child's reluctance. You can start by shortening the distance to see if interest awakens again. If not, let her sit and relax, or move on to another activity.

This activity promotes: Equality, Self-esteem, Timing, Cooperation

Giving your child the choice, when and if to submerge, as early as possible is positive in many ways. I certainly enjoy activities more when it is my choice to do them, don't you? It makes the activity more equal and by respecting a child's choice means respecting the child's integrity, too. When you respect your child's integrity, your baby's self-esteem grows.

The Mini Penguin Plunge

Charming little penguins happily plunge into the water... your baby can do this motion too, once she is able to sit. She'll do the Mini Penguin Plunge, with your support, as she goes from sitting on the deck to confidently plunging into the water and gliding into your arms. (If the distance between the deck and surface of the water is far then an alternative may be for her to sit on a pool mat or the stairs.)

1. Your child sits on the pool deck with her legs in the water.
2. You stand in front of her with your shoulders in the water.
3. Let her hold your hands; alternatively, place your hands under her arms and around her chest.
4. Make eye contact with her and communicate what is about to happen so she can get ready to enter the water.
5. Guide her with your voice, clear mimicry and your hands, so she leans forward into the water with a continuous sliding motion. Be careful not to create waves and stay steady, so your baby can maintain balance as she swims the short distance to you.
6. Finish the swim by letting your child rest on your hands, or with her tummy on your chest, meeting her face to face.
7. Watch her reaction and be ready to respond and celebrate the new experience together.
8. When you believe she is ready, return to the wall by swimming on the surface. Support your child with the position, The Scout (page 153). Because children learn from experience, it's a great idea to make a habit of always returning back to the wall and repeating the process over and over again.

The first time you do this activity, you may find that it is difficult to achieve eye contact with your little one. While sitting on the deck, your child may take interest in something else around her, as the world is so exciting and new. If this happens, simply give her some time to look around and talk about the new experience she is having. When she is ready, she will direct her attention to you and make eye contact when you call on her. If it takes too long then lift her gently back down into the warm water and return her to the deck ready to retry the activity from the start.

Make sure you allow your child to go below the surface of the water. Follow her motion, just as if she were moving independently. Keep her balanced and, if needed, guide her up toward you. You must give your child as true an experience as possible, as that is how she will learn to do it on her own when she is able. Your child will become a skilled swimmer gradually, with your support and guidance.

In doing this, you give your child full initiative and you'll see how she will further develop her swimming skills of entering the water and finding balance, with happiness. Your child is now fully aware that she is going under the water and therefore there is no need for you to give her a submerge signal anymore; a clear invitation is enough.

If your child does not want to participate in this activity, lift her up and clearly say to her, "I see you and understand that you do not want to do this right now and that is okay."

This activity promotes: Leadership, Communication, Trust, Self-Sufficiency, Joy

Caution

Some children try to enter the water by scooting their bottoms to the edge of the pool and falling in feet first. Don't let your baby do this! There is a great a risk of your child hitting the back of her head on the deck, when trying to enter the pool in this manner. If your child tries this, stop her, and help by guiding her to make a safer entrance into the water so that her head (the heaviest part of her body) is forward and over the water.

The Big Penguin Plunge

After mastering The Mini Penguin Plunge, a child that is able to stand by himself is ready for the next advanced activity.

1. Support your little one with one hand as he stands on the deck.
2. Stand in the water to the side of your child and close to the wall. This allows you to support him while you leave an open space for him to jump into the water.
3. Invite your child to jump in. Wait for him to take the initiative.

IMPORTANT
Small children do not have a very strong launch to begin with when they jump into the pool, which means that you have to be ready to take their hand and make sure they get far enough away from the wall to ensure safety. Encourage your child to jump far out. Keep supporting your child when he jumps until you are sure that he is able to make a long launch himself.

After the jump, you can soften the downward force that will naturally occur when he jumps into the water, once your child is under the water's surface.
Then either guide him up, or if he knows his way, let him swim back to the surface to you. When your child seems ready, let him complete this activity by swimming back to the wall using The Free Swim (page 173) or The Royal Launch (page 174).

This activity promotes: Leadership, Communication, Trust, Resilience, Joy

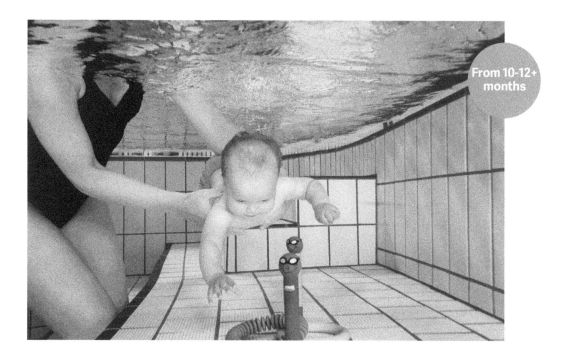

From 10-12+ months

Treasure Hunt

Toys that sink can easily pique your child's interest. How the toy(s) sinks to the bottom of a pool is fascinating and provides a science lesson inviting children to explore and understand the basic laws of physics through play.

Share in your child's amazement and ask if she can try to retrieve a toy once it sinks. Some children will want to see you do it first so they can copy, while others will try first, reacting with surprise and happiness when they succeed.

If your child needs to see it done first (as many will), I recommend you start by placing the toy in shallow water (the stairs, for example), and increasing the challenge gradually by placing the toy at greater depths of water. It will be a joy for you to watch her explore the underwater world and the and magic she is discovering.

Your child will clearly communicate if it's too difficult by turning away from it. If it's just right, she will show her interest and try herself or signal for a little help.

Give her just the right amount of support, and gradually let her take over as her ability and skills grow. This way your baby will feel success and gain more confidence to try new things while you are also nurturing your baby's love of learning.

In this activity, your child learns to go under the surface of the water and orient herself, grab an object and return up again. Your child will discover that buoyancy makes it difficult for her to go down deep and because of this, in the beginning, she needs your help. In this way, it will become a collaborative activity.

This activity promotes: Discovery, Interest/ Awareness, Focus

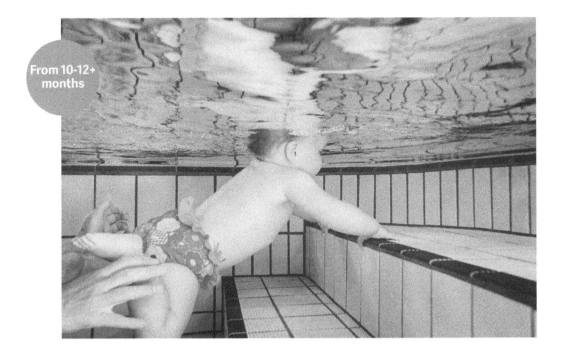

From 10-12+ months

Mini Swims From and Toward the Stairs

Swimming to and from the stairs is another activity that supports your child's natural development toward independence. This activity also offers an easy and natural way for him to practice getting in and out of the water together with you.

Note: He may need to hold onto your hands at first. Remember not to pull but rather gently guide and support his swim through the water, making sure he wants to follow you and not forcing the swim.

From the stairs:
1. Your child sits, tummy deep, on the stairs.
2. You stand in front of him.
3. When ready, invite him to swim toward you. If the distance is right for him, he will swim out to your waiting hands.

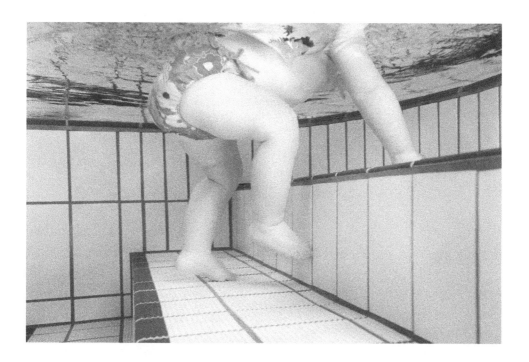

To the stairs:

1. Stand near the stairs and make sure you each have a clear target to where your baby should swim.
2. He will be on his tummy and you'll support him like in The Scout (page 153).
3. When ready, communicate, "Are you ready to swim to the stairs?" .
4. When and if he is ready, let him slide down under the surface and swim towards the stairs.
5. Watch your child closely during his swim and help him find his way if he seems to need it.
6. Let him complete this activity, if he is up for it, by crawling up the stairs.

Note: He can also take off by himself, using The Royal Launch (page 174).

For a baby, self-sufficiency is a delight. If you help him with step-by-step support, gradually he'll be able to do things on his own, developing resilience and feeling challenged to further develop his skills in and out of the water.

This activity promotes: Self-Sufficiency, Motor Development, Confidence, Resilience

The Baby Cannonball

From the age of one, children have a stronger need to tumble, jump and swing. These activities develop their motor skills and strengthen the muscles in their growing bodies. In the water, it is possible to do activities you would never do on land for fear of injury. The Baby Cannonball is one of these activities and it requires a second adult to support the activity.

Be aware of how much excitement your child can handle and proceed accordingly. I recommend you start small and expand gradually, always taking responsibility and prioritizing your child's needs.

1. Let your child squat and have her feet in the palm of your hands as she faces the other adult.
2. When ready, the other adult invites your child to jump.
3. Wait for the launch as your little one jumps up and forward toward the adult in front of her.
4. Your baby jumps over, or into the water, and will make a short swim before reaching the adult. Distance depends on your child's preference, experience and skill level.
5. Start with short jumps and cooperate with the child to gradually increase the distance.

Always make sure it is safe for him and those around you (i.e., do not do this close to other people or close to the wall/steps of the pool). You want to do this activity in deeper water, so that there is no fear of touching the bottom of the pool upon landing.

This activity promotes: Cooperation, Multiple Sensory Input, Emotional Development

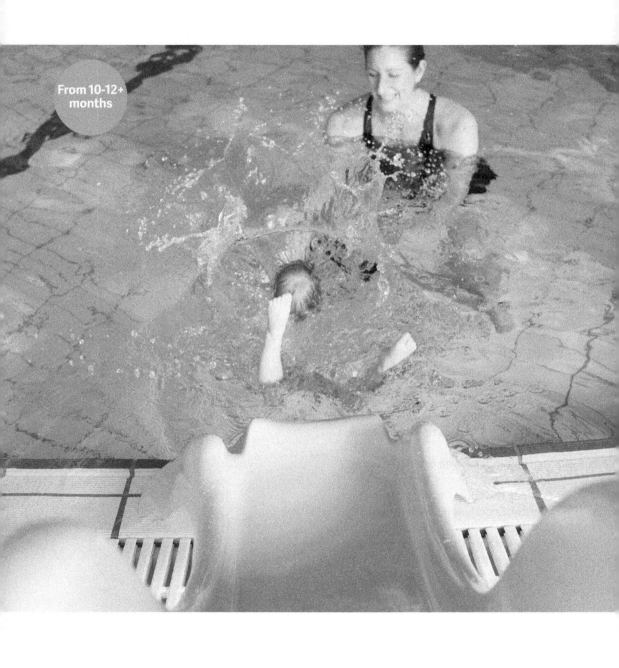

From 10-12+ months

The Happy Slide Ride

Many children love slides and sliding into the water is just as fun! If you are lucky enough that your pool has a slide that is safe for children then this activity can provide additional joy.

I strongly recommend making a habit of teaching your child to slide into the swimming pool head-first and on his tummy.

There are two reasons for this:

1. **Safety**. The slide will become slippery and the ride will therefore be fast. Your little one might not yet have the strength to lean forward at the end as he enters the water, which can make hitting his head a risk. Being on his tummy avoids this problem.

2. **Ease of swimming**. Riding down head-first on the tummy gives your child a natural glide forward once he enters the water, allowing him to swim to the person waiting for him in the water.

Many children do not want to lie on their tummy during their first trip down a slide. You might encounter him saying something like, "Thanks, but no thanks!" and that's okay. It's understandably a little nerve-wracking for a child to go down a slide in this way. Give him time to build his courage and your child's desire to try this position will eventually outweigh his fear.

After the first trip down the slide, some children are ready to repeat the process and practice the activity. For other children, one trip will be enough until their desire pulls them towards it again. My advice is to go slowly in the beginning and try to reduce your child's speed the first few times they do this activity. The more comfortable your child feels, the better the outcome for future slide rides.

After the first ride you will probably see if your child requires more or less support and you can adjust accordingly. If you allow your child to use the slide at his own pace, he will soon love it, and it will expose him to a series of beneficial sensations and challenges.

When your child uses the slide, you will need the help of another adult until he can safely climb up the stairs by himself.

1. The helper helps your child onto the slide and stays by him.
2. Your child should be lying on his tummy with his head pointing down toward the water.
3. You stand in the water a couple of feet from the end of the slide, ready to move away or toward the slide.
4. Make sure that all three of you are ready for the launch: "Ready? Then we slide down to...!"
5. The helper on deck stays beside your child and supports him (physically and mentally) during his entire trip down the slide. Adjust the speed and be mindful to control your child's landing into the water.
6. Once your child is in the water, he will swim up to you or you will gently guide him back up to the water's surface and to you.
7. When, and if, your baby is ready, help him swim back to the wall again.

Once your child is confident doing this activity and is better at balancing after entering the water, you can give him room to expand it by letting him slide down himself and swim further out to you.

This activity promotes: Emotional Development, Cooperation, Self-Sufficiency, Joy

Carousel Dive

This is an extension and variation of The Carousel Ride (see page 156). You can introduce this activity when your child is comfortable under the water and enjoys a little speed.

1. Start with your child laying on his tummy, resting his chest on your extended forearm. You may want to keep a gentle hold of his distant upper arm.
2. Use your other arm to support him under his thighs.
3. Turn around in a circle in the same direction as your child is looking.
4. As you move, check in with him so he is engaged and to determine if he is ready for more.
5. When ready, lift him out of the water and ask if he is ready to go under water.
6. Still moving in a circle, let your child submerge under the water in a gliding movement as he continues to rest on your arms.
7. After taking a little spin under the water, your child continues to gently glide up to the surface of the water again.

In the beginning always go slowly so it's easy for your child to follow and for you to stop the activity if it becomes too much for him. When you and your child are ready for more, gradually move faster and/or higher!

This activity promotes: Leadership, Responsiveness, Fun

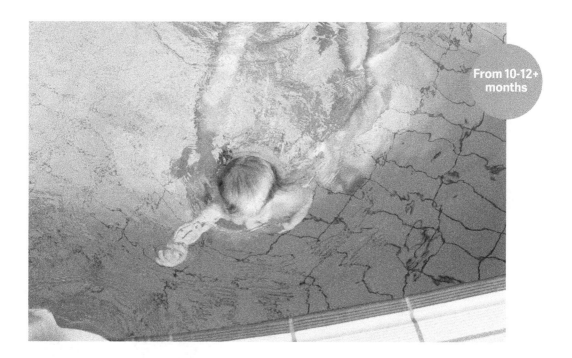

Expand The Happy Slide Ride
to Include Swimming Back to the Wall or Stairs

Once your baby gets used to going down the slide, she will probably start taking the initiative to return to the wall, or the stairs, so that she can go again! Keep an eye out for this development and support it. It will give your little one an opportunity to develop her swimming skills.

This activity promotes: Cooperation, Confidence, Competence, Resilience

From 10-12+ months

Climb out, jump in, swim back

I Can Do It Myself!

One great part of childhood is when the child feels good support, from empathetic parents, so that they can gradually grow from dependant to independent.

During the second year of your child's life, he has learned to move independently around on land. He needs the same freedom in the water, with some adjustments to ensure his safety.

The basic swimming skills that your child learns can be combined to satisfy his need for more independence. These swimming combinations also give your child a sense that he can accomplish things by himself.

Between the ages of one and two, a child can learn to jump into the water, swim to the wall and climb up out of the pool all by himself. The swimming distance can vary from just a short distance to much longer.

Here is a summary of the basic skills that may be in your child's repertoire when you get to this point of swimming:

1. Entering the water from the deck either from the sitting or standing position, or from The Mini Penguin Plunge (page 177), or The Big Penguin Plunge (page 178).
2. Turning around underwater.
3. Swimming back to the wall.
4. Gripping and holding onto the wall.
5. Climbing out of the pool onto the deck.

Once your child has mastered these tasks individually, you will either see him combine them into sequences or you can guide him into how to combine different moves. Nurture your child's interest with an appropriate level of step-by-step support and give him a chance to practice different combinations with you.

Keep in mind that it's a good lesson to have your baby experience trial and error, as long as the struggle is manageable for him. Allow your child to do as much as he can on his own. When the cooperation between you both is effective, and you give him room to explore, your child will feel that you support and trust in his ability to learn, and he will discover that he can do it! This realization will cause him to beam with pride and confidence, ready to take on more of life's challenges in many aspects of life.

This activity promotes: Self-Esteem, Competence, Confidence, Resilience

Swimming Is Part of Life's Journey

The ability to swim is essential. We are drawn to water and we live on a planet whose surface is more than 70% water. When you give your child with the gift of swim, you are helping them to develop skills for life—skills that will make them more equipped for life on Earth. Depending on where you live, familiarity with water can be vital, even if you don't swim in the ocean or a pool. Water is life, water is fun and water demands awareness, so make friends with it.

For anyone who reads this book and is still hesitant about baby swimming, look at it this way: You can build a fence around the pool, you can make your child wear a life jacket twenty-four hours a day, and you can forbid your child to ever to go near water and try to monitor her behavior constantly. But a day will come when your child breaks the rules, so my best advice is to teach her to swim and take the precautions that make her as safe as possible. After all, you will not be able to shield her from every social activity that involves proximity to water.

As a parent, the best thing you can do is guide her well and give her the opportunity to live in our wonderful world, to live *life*—and water is part of that. The more time you spend in the water together, the more you learn not only about its possibilities and limitations, but your possibilities as well. You'll also develop a sound knowledge about your child's abilities and need of your attention.

Water is also an emotional journey. People have an emotional connection to it. Some may feel at peace near the water. Others may be fearful of rough seas. No matter your personal view, there is an emotional response to water and it's important to recognize this.

Throughout this book, I've talked about baby swimming and my model of letting your relationship with your child, and your child's needs, guide how to learn swimming together. By introducing your baby to swim in this way, you and your child will grow together in many ways towards happiness in the water, and outside of the water, too.

We've covered many topics, so to recap, here are important points to keep in mind while you embark on the wonderful adventure of swimming with your baby.

- A child's actions always have meaning. When you tune-in to your child you can give your baby a head-start in many aspects of their developmental growth, through swim.

- Learning together has amazing effects. In my classes, I considered the parents (or other caregivers) the students, as much as the babies. When the parents can acknowledge that they are also students who need to learn and grow, the most profound impact can take place through the joint experience of swimming.

- Adults taking responsibility and leadership in the relationship is the key to developing secure attachments and trust. When you are able to see the world through your child's eyes, the world you are guiding your baby through makes a lot more sense and will be easier for you to guide her through it.

- Respecting your child's integrity and finding equal dignity is crucial for a healthy, happy relationship. This is a topic that is nuanced, but so life-changing when done properly. It goes back to respecting a child's needs and finding a happy medium that respects your child's wishes (as indeed they are always trying to tell you something) while also keeping them safe and acting in their best interest (which only you as the leader can know and do!).

- Lastly, we covered the topics of building the foundation for resilience and the subject of how emotional intelligence can help guide situations in and out of the water. These life lessons are imperative and lead to happy babies, happy parents and happy families.

Childhood is a journey toward independence, self-awareness and self-sufficiency, three characteristics that will help your child in all aspects of life. The key to achieving this is providing predictable, responsive and caring support to your child throughout childhood. This helps the child develop confidence in themselves and in others that they love and trust.

When a baby takes a journey with a supportive parent, they end up being a healthy and happy baby! This parent keeps the child safe, shows the child life lessons, shares in the activities, trusts in their learning, and is present to experience the ups, downs and in-betweens, always by their side.

When a child has someone that really believes in them, and shows them support time and time again, what a child can accomplish is endless!

The next step is for you to implement these life lessons in the water. My greatest wish is for every parent, guardian and caregiver—around the world—to give their babies the gift of swim. When done the right way, with the relationship between you and your baby as the priority, happiness comes to all involved.

You can find more information on me and how to swim with your baby at www.ulrika.us

Happy swimming!

References

The Harvard Study of Adult Development (Triumphs of Experience, sharing more
findings from the Grant Study 2012) Vailliant, George (Present Director of the study:
Dr. Robert J. Waldinger)

The Early-Years Swimming Research Project, Final report 2013, Professor Robyn
Jorgensen

The Development of the Person: The Minnesota Study of Risk and Adaptation from
Birth to Adulthood 2005 Dr. Alan Sroufe, Institute for Child Development at the
University of Minnesota

Center on the Developing Child Harvard University (see under useful links page 196)

Baby Bonds: Parenting, attachment and a secure base for children, 2014, published and
funded by the Sutton Trust

Acknowledgments

The fact that this book has finally been published humbles me and fills me with gratitude, and I want to take the opportunity to express my thanks:

A big, warm thank you the most awesome editor, Susie M. Haley, who with enthusiasm and professionalism took on the job and went above and beyond. This book would not have been the same without you. Thank you for pushing it further. You transformed my dream into a fantastic read and gave it the best title I could wish for. I am forever grateful.

Bryn Mohr thank you for your friendship, your everlasting wonderful support and careful and excellent proofreading.

Mette Schou at Gipsy Graphics, whose creativity made this a beautiful book.

Photographers Daniel Stjerne and Tuala Hjarnø, for capturing the incredible moments in lovely pictures. And thanks to the children and parents who took the time to attend the photo sessions—it's a prettier book because of you.

Pediatrician Jørgen Diderichsen, for making necessary corrections to the material on child development and special medical considerations.

Dave Dubois, a never-ending source of support, inspiration and knowledge in the aquatic arena. Gudrun Gjesing, a wizard on the subject of children's perceptions and physical development. Anna-Sofie Rønde Nørgaard and Dorte Eilsø, I always treasure our talks and reflections on psychology, pedagogics and swimming, and how to put it into great practice! Thank you to all four for your valuable comments on the book and your encouragement, support and friendship.

A big warm thank you to Jesper Juul and the Family lab team: I am grateful for the learning and growth I've had with you knowledgeable, experienced and warm-hearted people.

Friends and colleagues all over the world: Thank you for being YOU and for your encouragement, and also for your courage in changing the world for our little ones and their families into something gentle, nourishing and happy.

My husband, Johan Faerch: Thank you for your love and support and for always believing in me. And our children, Auguste and Ida Victoria: You make me both tender, strong and proud. I never stop feeling lucky to have you in my life.

And last, but not least, to all past and future children and parents—you are a source of inspiration, learning and joy. Thank you for the trust and opportunity you give us swim teachers to follow and guide your journey—I wish you all the best and an ocean full of great experiences in the waters you play in.

Recommended Reading

Additional books on baby swimming and learning to swim:

Baby Swimming by Lilli Ahrendt (Meyer & Meyer Sport, 2002)

Learn to Swim by Rob and Cathy McKay (DK Adult, 2005)

Teaching Your Baby to Swim by Françoise Barbira Freedman (Lorenz Books, 2012)

Water Babies: Teach Your Baby the Joys of Water—from Newborn Floating to Toddler Swimming by Françoise Barbira Freedman (Anness, 2001)

Books, not specific to baby swimming, that have inspired and influenced my work:

Attachment-Focused Parenting: Effective strategies to Care for Children by Daniel A. Hughes (W.W. Norton & Company, 2009)

Born for Love: Why Empathy Is Essential—and Endangered by Bruce D. Perry and Maia Szalavitz (William Morrow Paperbacks, 2011)

The Boy Who Was Raised as a Dog: And Other Stories from a Child Psychiatrist's Notebook by Bruce D. Perry and Maia Szalavitz (Basic Books, 2017)

Childism: Confronting Prejudice Against Children by Elisabeth Young-Bruehl (Yale University Press, 2013)

Diary of a Baby: What Your Child Sees, Feels, and Experiences by Daniel N. Stern (Basic Books, 1992)

Ethics in Light of Childhood by John Wall (Georgetown University Press, 2010)

The Explosive Child: A New Approach for Understanding and Parenting Easily Frustrated, Chronically Inflexible Children by Ross W. Greene (Harper Paperbacks, 2014)

Here I Am! Who are You?: Resolving Conflicts Between Adults and Children by Jesper Juul (AuthorHouse UK, 2012)

Hold On to Your Kids: Why Parents Need to Matter More than Peers by Gordon Neufeld and Gabor Maté (Ballantine Books, 2006)

I and Thou by Martin Buber (Touchstone, 1971)

The Interpersonal World of the Infant: A View from Psychoanalysis and Development by Daniel N. Stern (Basic Books, 2000)

Relational Competence: Towards a New Culture of Education by Jesper Juul and Helle Jensen (edition + plus, 2017)

A Secure Base: Parent-Child Attachment and Healthy Human Development by John Bowlby (Basic Books, 1988)

Your Competent Child: Toward a New Paradigm in Parenting and Education by Jesper Juul (Balboa Press, 2011)

Also the following books published in Swedish:

Anknytning i Praktiken ["Attachment in practice"] by Anders Broberg, Pehr Granqvist, Tord Ivarsson, and Pia Risholm Mothander (Natur & Kultur, 2008)

Anknytningsteori ["Attachment theory"] by Anders Broberg, Pia Risholm Mothander, Pehr Granqvist, and Tord Ivarsson (Natur & Kultur, 2006)

Utvecklingspsykologi ["Developmental psychology"] by Leif Havnesköld and Pia Risholm Mothander (Liber, 2009)

Utvecklingspsykologi ["Developmental psychology"] by Philip Hwang and Björn Nilsson (Natur & Kultur, 2011)

Useful and inspiring links:

"Baby Swimming: Exploring the Effects of Early Intervention on Subsequent Motor Abilities"
https://www.researchgate.net/publication/26779487_Baby_swimming_exploring_the_effects_of_early_intervention_on_subsequent_motor_abilities

"Early Years Swimming: Adding Capital to Young Australians"
https://docs.wixstatic.com/ugd/438ac6_ab695f7ad49f4decb7a2a3c9db453b6c.pdf

"Pilot Study on Infant Swimming Classes and Early Motor Development"
https://www.ncbi.nlm.nih.gov/labs/articles/24665810/

Center on the Developing Child Harvard University
https://developingchild.harvard.edu/

Lives in the Balance Fostering (Ross W. Greene)
https://www.livesinthebalance.org/

Safer 3 message—Recognize the risks of a drowning event and implementing the resources to reduce the risks.
https://www.stopdrowningnow.org

'NO DROWN TOWN' The concept is built around the idea of encouraging individuals and families to make their homes a 'NO DROWN TOWN', using the Safer Swimming 'layers of protection' message to take care of those closest to them.
https://australianswimschools.org.au/community/no-drown-town/

UN Convention on the Rights of the Child
https://www.unicef.org/crc/

UN Convention on the Rights of the Child in Child-Friendly Language
https://www.unicef.org/rightsite/files/uncrcchilldfriendlylanguage.pdf

"It's not about reaching the destination, it's the journey you take together that brings you happiness."

ISBN: 1719244057
ISBN-13: 978-1719244053

Editor: Susie M Haley
Art Director: Mette Schou
Photographers: Tuala Hjarnø and Daniel Stjerne

The website addresses referred to in this book were correct at the time
of publication.

Lightning Source UK Ltd.
Milton Keynes UK
UKHW05f1829140918
328919UK00007B/660/P